"Our children are going to lear[...] downright evil voices or from [...] moms and dads are often hard pressed to [...] these sensitive matters. *Helping Your Kids Know God's Good Design* is a biblically grounded, down-to-earth, personalized, wisdom-filled resource for parents, who will appreciate that it does not shy away from addressing the most difficult, highly charged, intimate issues. Highly recommended!"

—**Gregg Allison**, professor of Christian Theology, The Southern
Baptist Theological Seminary; secretary, Evangelical Theological Society;
and senior fellow, Ethics and Religious Liberty Commission

"Helping your child navigate the land mines related to sexuality and gender is a daunting task in today's world. Elizabeth tackles tough topics with humility, relying on the timeless, trustworthy Word of God. She gives parents practical tools to point their children to the truth and beauty of God's perfect wisdom and design."

—**Nancy DeMoss Wolgemuth**, author; founder/Bible teacher, Revive Our Hearts

"There has been a longtime need for a book like this. After all, we want to talk with our kids about sex but are often at a loss how to do so. Urbanowicz offers a biblically informed and practical guide for helping parents talk with their kids wisely about sex. You can read it straight through or use it as a guide when tough questions arise. I highly recommend parents read this book and discuss it together."

—**Sean McDowell, PhD**, is a professor of apologetics at Biola
University, the author of *Chasing Love*, and a popular YouTuber

"*Helping Your Kids Know God's Good Design* is a biblical, thoughtful, clear, compassionate, practical, and altogether excellent resource for parents. Whether your children are toddlers or teenagers, Elizabeth's book will equip you to answer their questions and show them God's beautiful plan for gender and sexuality."

—**Neil Shenvi, (AB, PhD)**, author of *Why Believe?*, *Critical Dilemma*, and *Post Woke*

"*Helping Your Kids Know God's Good Design* is the most practical book on teaching sexuality to children I have seen. It removes the fear factor for parents and equips them to have conversations that count. A much-needed resource!"

—**Israel Wayne**, author, speaker, and founder of FamilyRenewal.org

HELPING YOUR KIDS KNOW GOD'S GOOD DESIGN

Elizabeth Urbanowicz

HARVEST APOLOGETICS
AN IMPRINT OF HARVEST HOUSE PUBLISHERS

Cover design by Faceout Studio, Spencer Fuller
Custom cover imagery created by Faceout Studio.
Interior design by KUHN Design Group

For bulk, special sales, or ministry purchases, please call 1-800-547-8979. Email: CustomerService@hhpbooks.com

H| This logo is a trademark of the Hawkins Children's LLC. Harvest House Publishers, Inc., is the exclusive licensee of this trademark.

Helping Your Kids Know God's Good Design
Copyright © 2025 by Elizabeth Urbanowicz
Published by Harvest House Publishers
Eugene, Oregon 97408
www.harvesthousepublishers.com

ISBN 978-0-7369-9139-1 (pbk)
ISBN 978-0-7369-9140-7 (eBook)

Library of Congress Control Number: 2025930241

Printed in the United States of America

25 26 27 28 29 30 31 32 33 / BP / 10 9 8 7 6 5 4 3 2 1

To Pastor Dennis Burns

*Without your faithful discipleship, Foundation Worldview
would not exist, and neither would this book. Thank you for
shepherding the flock God entrusted to you with fierce gentleness.*

CONTENTS

PART 3: ADDRESSING ANXIETIES AND FEARS

PART 4: WHEN LOVED ONES ARE LIVING OUTSIDE OF GOD'S DESIGN

PART 5: EVERYDAY QUESTIONS AND CONVERSATIONS

INTRODUCTION

Not long ago, I took a friend's children to our neighborhood playground. There, I overheard a conversation taking place between two fifth-grade girls on the swings. "It's so ridiculous that she doesn't understand that not everyone is male or female," one girl said, sighing. She pumped her legs, trying to swing higher.

The other girl giggled as she twirled one of her braids. "I know. How ridiculous. She doesn't understand that some people are nonbinary?" The conversation continued, discussing the gender identities of different classmates, until the first girl dragged her legs in the dirt to slow her swing and asked, "Want to head back to my house for some ice cream?" As the two girls walked down the sidewalk, I watched, shocked over the dramatic cultural shift I had just witnessed firsthand. And this shift is probably one of the main reasons you have picked up this book.

No longer do we live in a world where kids are simply free to be kids. From an early age, the world around them pushes highly sexualized content in their faces. In fact, by the time our children reach the age where parents of decades past would typically have had "the talk," most of our children's peers will have already viewed pornography, been directly instructed about masturbation, and received hours' worth of exposure to the concept of gender identity. While this reality is somewhat terrifying, as Christians, it is vital that we not bury our heads in the sand, hoping our children will somehow be completely shielded from the world around them. Instead, we must take a proactive approach, grounding our children in the goodness of God's design before they are confronted with the world's endless corruptions. But how are we to do this? This question is something I have been studying for well over a decade.

In 2007, I began teaching fourth and then third grade at a Christian school just outside of Chicago. Though the cultural shift in beliefs about gender and sexuality was not as drastic back then, I still noticed that my students lacked the skills they needed to critically and biblically evaluate the countless secular ideas coming their way. Year after year, I watched as Christian influences at home, school, and church seemed to get washed away from students by the tides of culture. By my fifth year of teaching, I knew I could no longer simply watch this happen. I needed to equip my students to faithfully navigate the world around them. So when I couldn't find any materials to train them in the way I knew was necessary, I started creating resources of my own. An incredible shift occurred in my students' ability to think critically and biblically, which led people all over the country to reach out and request the resources I had created. I eventually realized the need I had identified in my students was a need that parents, teachers, and church leaders felt across the nation and the world. However, before seeking to publish any of the materials I had created, I felt compelled to first go back to school to earn a master's degree in Christian apologetics from Biola University (to ensure I truly knew what I was talking about). After completing that degree, I started Foundation Worldview, a ministry that seeks to equip Christian adults with practical resources for helping the children in their care carefully evaluate every idea they encounter and understand the truth of the biblical worldview.

Since its inception, over twenty thousand children have gone through a Foundation Worldview curriculum and have learned to think and live biblically in a secular culture. During this time, the number one request my team and I have received from parents is for resources to help ground their children in a biblical view of sexuality and gender. And I have written this book to do just that: guide you step-by-step through a host of foundational conversations to have with your child. Each chapter explores a particular question about sexuality or gender, and almost every question is one I have received directly from parents seeking guidance. While the topic of each question varies—from the ins and outs of "the talk," to preparing kids to interact with a family member who is transitioning, to everything in between—the flow of each conversation will take the same basic form.

In each chapter, we will first explore how to explain a positive biblically sound theology of the topic at hand. Then we will explore how sin has corrupted it. Starting such conversations with what is positive is vital because sexuality is an inherently good thing. God designed sex and gave it to us as a gift. It is not inherently dirty or shameful, and we want our children to know this. Only after they understand the goodness of God's design can we then convey how sin has corrupted it. If we flip the order, beginning such conversations with the corruption, our children's understanding of sexuality will be tainted, and they may never understand that God's design truly *is* good. Finally, at the end of each chapter, you will find a short summary paragraph recapping the key points that have been answered in our discussion.

The ultimate goal of each chapter is to provide a template for a particular conversation with your child. In most chapters, I have recommended a general age range in which to have this specific conversation. I have also sought to provide guidance for avoiding certain pitfalls, and suggestions for conversational modifications you can make depending on your child's personality. However, there is one thing to remember: *You* are the expert on your child. While I can provide general wise guidance for structuring and wording these conversations, God has given *you* the responsibility of being your child's primary disciple-maker. So if I suggest something, but you know it would need to be tweaked, added to, or left out of a conversation, please make that change. You are the expert on your child!

Another thing to note is that as you begin talking with your child about God's good design for sexuality, you may find yourself in a marriage or family situation that you never imagined or desired. Whether this is because of sinful choices you have made, the sin of others that has been thrust upon you, or simply the result of living in a fallen world, your situation may cause you to wonder how you can have these conversations with your child—especially when your life feels far from the goodness of God's design for marriage, sex, and family.

If this is you, know that I am right there with you. As I write these words, I am in my late thirties and still single. Singleness was never in my life plan. Not at 18. Not at 28. And definitely not at 38. But here I find myself, approaching 40 and still single. Though I know God's design for marriage, sex, and family are inherently good, God has not chosen to give me these good gifts in this season. And that fact brings with it a certain level of disappointment, longing, and grief.

You may be thinking, *Elizabeth, extended singleness cannot even begin to compare with the situation I am walking through!* And you may be right. I do not know the specifics of your situation. But here are two truths I do know—truths I hope you will keep at the forefront of your mind as you begin talking with your child about God's good design.

First, if you are a Christian, God has promised to use all things in your life, even painful and heart-wrenching situations, for your good. And his Word is clear about how he does this. God works all things together for good in the Christian's life by using all things to conform us more into the image of his Son (Romans 8:28-29). God has allowed you to be in this situation, in this moment, for your ultimate good. Whether your life looks very much like how you pictured it or nothing of the sort, God is using your current situation to make you more like Jesus.

Second, the ultimate goal of teaching our kids God's good design for sexuality is not to provide them with a picture-perfect marriage, sex life, or family. The ultimate goal of teaching our kids God's good design is for them to "taste and see that the LORD is good" (Psalm 34:8). It should be our prayer in this process that our children will turn from their sin and trust in Jesus, be reconciled to God, and have the hope of eternity with him in the new heaven and new earth, where sin and death will be no more (Mark 1:14-15; 2 Corinthians 5:20; Revelation 21:3-4). So, whether your current situation reflects the inherent beauty of God's good design or is light years from it, God has both called and equipped you to have these important conversations with your child. And he will use them for his glory and your good.

Now that I have revealed that I am single (and thus do not have children), you may be wondering what in the world I am doing writing a book instructing parents how to have conversations with their children. And that is a valid question. While I do not have firsthand experience parenting, my area of expertise is breaking down complex concepts into words, examples, and activities that kids as young as four years old can easily grasp. On top of this, one of the blessings of singleness is *time*. A mom of three young children may wonder how to wisely navigate the host of books at her local library pushing an LGBTQ+ agenda. Yet, amid changing diapers, tackling the never-ending mountain of laundry, refereeing sibling squabbles, and ensuring that everyone is fed and (at least mostly) clothed, she probably doesn't have long stretches of time to sit down and think over how to biblically guide her children through library trips. But as a single woman, I do (and we will cover this exact question in chapter 39). I am praying this gift of time God has given me, along with my expertise in communicating with kids, will bless you and your family.

As you make your way through this book, please remember to pray for your child. While it is vital to have the conversations outlined in each chapter intentionally, you cannot soften your child's heart or renew their mind. Only God can do that. So as you plan how and when to have different conversations about sexuality and gender, pray that God would prepare your child for each conversation and reveal himself to them. Pray that God would protect your child from the schemes of the enemy and the snares of the world, and graciously convict them of the sin that resides in their own heart. And as you do this, trust that God, your faithful heavenly Father, will guide you each step of the way.

Thank you, friend, for taking this first step on the journey of talking with your child about God's good design. I am praying that God meets you in the pages of this book and that you leave not only equipped to have these conversations with your child but also more in awe of God and his good design.

BIBLICAL FOUNDATION

What Is God's Good Design for Sex?

You are most likely reading this book because you desire to help your child grasp the goodness of God's design for sexuality. And that is exactly what we will cover in the following chapters. However, before we dive into talking with our children about the goodness of God's design, let's take a moment to ensure that we ourselves have a biblical understanding of it. Even if you already have a good grasp on this, taking time to review the biblical view of sexuality will only strengthen your ability to discuss it with your child.

The good news is that God's good design for sex and marriage is made clear right from the first few chapters of Genesis, and then it is confirmed throughout the Bible. From the initial chapters in Genesis, we can break down Scripture's teachings on sex and marriage into three main points:

1. Marriage is a lifelong covenant between one man and one woman

2. God designed sex as a good gift in marriage for intimacy and the creation of children

3. All forms of sex outside of a one-man-and-one-woman marriage covenant are sin

Let's take a closer look at the biblical background behind these principles.

1. MARRIAGE IS A LIFELONG COVENANT BETWEEN ONE MAN AND ONE WOMAN

We first see God's design for marriage in the second chapter of Genesis. Directly after creating woman out of man's rib, God leads Eve to Adam, giving her to him in marriage. Though we do not see a description of what we would typically recognize as a marriage ceremony, we know this is a marriage because a declaration is made: "Therefore a man shall leave his father and his mother and hold fast to his wife, and they shall become one flesh" (Genesis 2:24). The term *therefore* makes clear that God is instituting this pattern for the rest of humanity; moving forward, a man shall now leave his father and mother and hold fast to his wife, and they shall become one flesh. This pattern is then affirmed across multiple points throughout Scripture.

In Matthew 19, Jesus is questioned about marriage and divorce by the religious leaders. He responds by saying,

> Have you not read that he who created them from the beginning made them male and female, and said, "Therefore a man shall leave his father and his mother and hold fast to his wife, and the two shall become one flesh"? So they are no longer two but one flesh. What therefore God has joined together, let not man separate (verses 4-6).

Here, Jesus points back to Genesis 2, affirming what God established at the beginning of human history—that marriage is a lifelong covenant between one man and one woman.

This truth is again affirmed in Ephesians 5:22-33. In these verses, the apostle Paul reiterates the pattern of one man and one woman coming together in the covenant of marriage. He then explains that this covenant is meant to be a picture of Christ and the church. He writes,

> "Therefore a man shall leave his father and mother and hold fast to his wife, and the two shall become one flesh." This mystery is

profound, and I am saying that it refers to Christ and the church (verses 31-32).

Here Paul is confirming the pattern established in Genesis 2, but he takes it one step further by explaining that in its most complete sense, this union is a picture of the gospel, a picture of Christ and the church.

2. GOD DESIGNED SEX AS A GOOD GIFT IN MARRIAGE FOR INTIMACY AND THE CREATION OF CHILDREN

The opening chapters of Genesis not only provide us with the pattern for marriage but also show us the purpose for which God has given us the gift of sex. In Genesis 2:18, God looks upon Adam and says, "It is not good that the man should be alone; I will make him a helper fit for him." Some have taken this phrase to mean that Adam suffered from emotional loneliness, but that is not what this verse says. Adam was not lonely. He was alone, without a helper fit for him. What does this mean? Why would Adam need a helper when he already had God? The previous chapter in Genesis provides the answer. Genesis 1:28 says,

> God blessed them. And God said to them, "Be fruitful and multiply
> and fill the earth and subdue it, and have dominion over the fish
> of the sea and over the birds of the heavens and over every living
> thing that moves on the earth."

From this verse, we learn that the type of helper Adam needed was someone who could enable him to fulfill this command. While Adam could exercise dominion over creation with any other human, only with the creation of a woman could he multiply and fill the earth with children. These first chapters of Genesis make clear that marriage is the context for which God designed sex, and sex is the means God has given us to multiply and fill the earth.

Sex not only leads to the creation of children; sex also leads to intimacy. We see this in Genesis 4:1 when we read, "Adam *knew* Eve his wife, and she conceived and bore Cain" (emphasis added). In the original Hebrew, the verb *knew* is the word *yadah*, which is used frequently in the Old Testament as a euphemism for sexual intercourse between a husband and a wife. *Yadah* is also used to describe God's intimate knowledge of us. Psalm 139:1 says, "O LORD, you have searched me and *known* me" (emphasis added). Here again, the Hebrew word for *known* is *yadah*. The fact that the word *yadah* is consistently used as a euphemism for sexual intercourse between a husband and wife shows that one of God's purposes for sex within marriage is intimacy.

This pattern of sex leading to both children and intimacy is confirmed throughout Scripture. Psalm 127:3-4 says, "Behold, children are a heritage from the LORD, the fruit of the womb a reward. Like arrows in the hand of a warrior are the children of one's youth." Malachi 2:14-15 expands upon this truth:

> The LORD was witness between you and the wife of your youth,
> to whom you have been faithless, though she is your companion
> and your wife by covenant. Did he not make them one, with a
> portion of the Spirit in their union? And what was the one God
> seeking? Godly offspring. So guard yourselves in your spirit, and
> let none of you be faithless to the wife of your youth.

Song of Solomon, an entire book of the Bible, is a love poem between a husband and a wife, a bridegroom and a bride. Multiple chapters of this poem portray the husband and wife delighting in one another's bodies. In chapter 4, the groom delights in his bride, saying:

> You have captivated my heart, my sister, my bride;
> you have captivated my heart with one glance of your eyes,
> with one jewel of your necklace.
> How beautiful is your love, my sister, my bride!
> How much better is your love than wine,
> and the fragrance of your oils than any spice!
> Your lips drip nectar, my bride;
> honey and milk are under your tongue;

the fragrance of your garments is like the fragrance of Lebanon (verses 9-11).

These and many other passages throughout Scripture affirm the goodness of sexual intercourse within the context of marriage and how it was designed to lead to children and intimacy between a husband and a wife.

3. ALL FORMS OF SEX OUTSIDE OF A ONE-MAN-AND-ONE-WOMAN MARRIAGE COVENANT ARE SIN

The opening chapters of Genesis not only show us God's pattern and purpose for sex and marriage, but they also highlight how these good gifts have been tainted by sin. Genesis 3 outlines the fall of mankind into sin, and immediately in the next chapter, we see how quickly humans fall into sexual sin. In Genesis 4, we are told that Lamech takes two wives (Genesis 4:23-24). This is polygamy, which falls outside the pattern God established in the garden for marriage as a one-man-and-one-woman covenant. As the narrative in Genesis continues, we are not given a list of everything God considers sexual sin. However, in the following books of the Old Testament, what God considers sexual sin is made clear. When God gives the Ten Commandments to his people, he specifically states, "You shall not commit adultery" (Exodus 20:14). This means that sex outside of marriage is forbidden. Later, when the Mosaic Law is further explained in Leviticus, in chapter 18, God outlines every form of sexual intercourse that is considered a sin. As one reads through this list, it becomes clear that any form of sexual intercourse outside of marriage is sinful.

Here some may argue that many Old Testament marriages were polygamous. It is true that God made provisions in the Old Testament to allow for polygamy in certain circumstances. However, polygamy was never celebrated and was typically portrayed as something that led to difficulties and heartache (for example: Sarah and Hagar, Leah and Rachel, Hannah and Peninnah). In the New Testament, both Jesus and Paul point back to God's original design of marriage between one man and one woman (Matthew 19:4-6; Ephesians 5:31-33), and Paul affirms God's design when he explains that men who take on the role of elder in a church can only be the husband of one wife (1 Timothy 3:2; Titus 1:6).

The truth that any sexual activity outside of one man and one woman in the covenant of marriage is sinful is confirmed throughout the whole canon of Scripture. In Romans 1:18-32, Paul outlines how one of the consequences of human sin is God giving us over to our corrupt sexual desires. Hebrews 13:4 says, "Let marriage be held in honor among all, and let the marriage bed be undefiled, for God will judge the sexually immoral and adulterous." In 1 Corinthians 6:9-11, Paul describes sins that prevent someone from inheriting the kingdom of God, which include sexual immorality, adultery, and homosexuality. In verse 11, he writes, "Such were some of you. But you were washed, you were sanctified, you were justified in the name of the Lord Jesus Christ and by the Spirit of our God." Paul is saying that before someone comes to Christ, they may have been involved in many of these sins, but they are no longer to partake in such sins now that they have been cleansed. This again confirms that any form of sex outside of the one-man-and-one-woman marriage covenant is a sin.

* * *

God is the author of sex and marriage. He makes clear his design for these gifts in Scripture, and his design is good. Once we have a firm grasp on what Scripture teaches about sexuality, we are ready to begin having conversations with our children, helping them understand the goodness and beauty of God's design.

PART 1

HOW AND WHEN TO TALK ABOUT SEX

1

WHEN SHOULD I FIRST HAVE THE SEX TALK WITH MY CHILD?

Years ago, it was common for parents to have one awkward sex talk with their child, usually when the child was somewhere between the ages of eight and fourteen. If this is what you experienced growing up, you may want to make having "the talk" with your child less awkward but still believe that the traditional eight-to-fourteen age frame will work. I applaud you for desiring to make the sex talk less awkward, but I would encourage you not to wait to have this conversation until your child is eight or older. At Foundation Worldview, I recommend that parents start having the first of many sex talks with their children around the age of four. You may have read that last sentence and thought, *Oh my goodness! Are you kidding me, Elizabeth? Four years old?* But let me explain: I am not suggesting that you sit down with your four-year-old and talk through every single detail of the mechanics of sex. However, I am suggesting that to ensure your child understands the inherent goodness of God's design for sex, you need to begin this ongoing conversation before they are bombarded with lies from culture.

You have probably noticed that we live in a world that aggressively promotes an unbiblical vision of sexuality, even to the youngest of children. Not only does our world balk at the idea of reserving sex for marriage, but it also pushes the narrative that true freedom is the removal of all sexual boundaries.

This vision is being actively pushed upon our children through the books placed on shelves of the local library, the storylines written into children's shows and movies, the content that algorithms promote on our household devices, and the advertisements our children see on billboards and street corners. This means that if the world, with its faulty understanding of sexuality, educates our children before we do, our children's formative understanding of sex will be anything but biblical.

I know that sounds scary, and it is. However, as Christians, we need not give in to fear. Instead, we can intentionally and prayerfully use the tools God has given us to proactively prepare our children to understand the truth of God's good design and reject the lies of our culture. And part of this involves having conversations about sex with our children when they are young.

Have you ever noticed how the person you learned certain information from first naturally becomes the expert on that topic in your mind? My friend Hillary Ferrer from Mama Bear Apologetics pointed this out to me, and I think she is right. She has coined this phenomenon the "founder's effect." For example, to this day, I still view my dad as the ultimate expert on home repairs. Is this because he knows more about home repairs than anyone else? No. I view my dad as the expert because he was the first person to teach me those skills. As an adult, I am now acquainted with many more-skilled plumbers, painters, and HVAC technicians, but my dad is still the first person I call when I have a home repair question. It's similar with our children and how they understand sex. Whoever first introduces them to the concept of sex will naturally become the person they view as the expert, whether that person is you, a friend, a teacher, a cartoon character, a YouTube influencer, or even Google. If we want our children to be grounded in a biblical view of sexuality, we should encourage them to come to us first with their questions, curiosities, and fears. And for this to happen, we need to be the one who talks with them about sexuality first.

It's also important that we ensure our children's first understanding of the concept of sex is positive. After all, sexuality is a good gift from God, and we want our children to see it that way. However, if we hold off on such conversations until we are having them in response to an unbiblical vision of sexuality—after we have met a family with two dads, or after our unwed niece announces her pregnancy, or after a beloved children's show character starts explaining the concept of gender identity—we are thrust into backtracking. We must explain how these things do not align with God's good design before our children even understand what that design is. When we are forced to backtrack, our children's first exposure to the concept of sexuality is grounded in how humans have corrupted the gift of sex rather than the inherent goodness of God's design. This will taint how they understand this good gift. Instead, we want to first ground our children in an understanding that sex within the covenant of marriage is inherently good.

When we begin these conversations with our four-year-olds, our words should mainly be focused on introducing key vocabulary, providing some necessary details, and grounding the concept of sex in the goodness of God's design. We want our little ones to understand the basics and know that sex is not dirty but a good gift from God. At the same time, we want them to see that sex isn't something that should be shared with everyone because it is a special gift designed to be shared only between a husband and a wife. (I will provide more details on how you can have these conversations in the following chapter.)

In these early conversations, we are also helping our children understand the boundaries God has placed on sex. This plants seeds of understanding regarding when those boundaries are being crossed. As we teach children that these boundaries are designed to keep us safe, we are also teaching them how God's good gift of sex can be misused when taken outside of those boundaries, including when it comes to pornography and sexual abuse. We will get into these topics more in-depth, but for now, it's good for us to know that giving children the language and wisdom to recognize when sex is being misused is an important way to keep their hearts, minds, and bodies safe. This is one more reason why having these conversations about sex early is so important!

Right now, you might be reading this and thinking, *My child is way older than four, and I haven't started having these conversations. Is it already too late?* My response to this is a resounding no! No matter how old your child is, these conversations are valuable. Talking about sex with your child is the only way to ensure they understand the goodness of God's design, and such conversations help them feel safe and comfortable coming to you with their questions rather than turning to the internet or their peers. The way you approach a conversation about sex with your nine-year-old will be different from your approach with your four-year-old, and we will discuss the details of that in the following chapters. But it is never too late to start these important conversations.

• • •

Helping our children have a biblical view of sex involves much more than one awkward sex talk. Ideally, we should have ongoing conversations about sex that begin at an early age. Though this concept may be new or overwhelming, with the proper preparation, such conversations need not be awkward or embarrassing. So if you are ready to proactively talk with your child about God's good design for sex, please keep reading. In the next chapter, we will get into the specifics.

2

WHAT SHOULD I COVER WHEN I TALK WITH MY CHILD ABOUT SEX?

When you think about having the first sex talk with your child, how do you feel? Fearful? Anxious? Panicked? Uncertain? Confused? If any of these words describe you, you are not alone. Starting the conversation about sex with our children can feel intimidating, mainly because we are unsure of what needs to be covered and how to explain it in a developmentally appropriate way. Anytime we are unprepared for something, we naturally feel more anxious. However, proper preparation, planning, and prayer lead to greater confidence and peace.

For the remainder of this chapter, I want to walk you through how to have a series of developmentally appropriate sex talks with a child between the ages of four and seven. If your child is over the age of seven, you can still glean wisdom from this chapter. However, I recommend that you also reference chapter 5, which will cover what to do if your first sex talk is taking place when your child is at an older age.

1. TALKING ABOUT BODY PARTS

Before we explain the act of sexual intercourse to our children, they need to understand the basics of male and female anatomy—so our first conversation should be about these different body parts. An easy way to begin is to ask your child about their favorite toy. Ask what they like about this toy and how they treat it differently than other toys. Discuss how your child is careful with how and when they play with this toy, and how they don't let just anyone play with it. Then you can explain that just as they treat this special toy with care, God has given us special body parts to treat with care.

Then take your child to Genesis 1:27, which reads, "God created man in his own image, in the image of God he created him; male and female he created them." You can ask your child what the final part of this verse reveals about how God created us. Then discuss how God created us as male or female. You can say, "*Male* is a fancy word for *boy*, and *female* is a fancy word for *girl*." Explain that as soon as your child was born, you knew whether they were male or female, and you knew this by looking at the special part of their body God had created.

If you have never introduced the anatomically correct words for genitalia, this is the time to do so. For example, you could say, "God designed you as a boy. So the special part of your body is called your penis." Or: "God designed you as a girl. So the special part of your body is called your vagina." Then you can explain the genitalia God created for the opposite sex. If your child has a younger sibling of the opposite sex, they've most likely bathed with this sibling or seen their diaper being changed, so this should be an easy conversation. If not, you will want to accompany this conversation with a basic illustration. A helpful resource for this is *The Story of Me* by Stan and Brenna Jones. This book contains simple illustrations that show both male and female genitalia in a developmentally appropriate way.

You can then say, "Most of the time, you probably won't notice this part of your body except when you use the bathroom. Boys pass urine through their penis. Girls do not pass urine through their vagina, but their vagina is a part of the body they wipe after urinating." Then explain that God designed these parts of the male and female body for another very special purpose that you will talk about in the future. At this point, you can end the conversation by asking your child if he or she has any questions. I know this can be intimidating because you don't know what questions they might ask, but you don't need to worry. If your child asks you a question that shocks, surprises, or confuses you, or if they ask a question you just don't know the answer to, you can respond by saying, "That's a great question. I'm so thankful you are thinking deeply about our conversation. I'll need a little time to answer that question, but we can talk more about it tomorrow [or tonight, or any time in the next 48 hours that works]."

2. TALKING ABOUT SEX

This next conversation may be one of the most uncomfortable ones you'll have with your child. However, the great thing about beginning these conversations when your child is young is that only one person in the conversation will feel any discomfort, and that's you. For most children, the topic of sex doesn't feel embarrassing or uncomfortable until they're around the age of eight. So my recommendation for approaching this conversation is to take a deep breath, put on a smile, and walk forward with a clear game plan.

When we introduce the concept of sex to our children, our goal should be to present sex as an inherently good part of God's design for the covenant of marriage. We do not want to present sex as the purpose of a marriage, but rather as an act designed specifically *for* marriage. A simple way to open this conversation is to ask your child if they have ever made a promise to someone. Discuss what kind of promises they have made. If they have never made a promise, you can share some promises you have made, such as promising to take them to the park or promising to bring home a treat. Then you can talk about how when people make a promise, they sometimes shake hands, lock pinkies, or even sign a contract. All of these actions show that a promise is serious, and the people making it plan to keep it.

You can then say, "Did you know that marriage is a promise? When a husband and wife get married, they promise to love one another in a way that they do not love anyone else. And they promise to stay together for their whole lives." You can then take your child to Genesis 2:24, which reads, "Therefore a man shall leave his father and his mother and hold fast to his wife, and they shall become one flesh." You can read the verse a second time and ask your child to listen to what truth is revealed at the end. When your child identifies "becoming one flesh" as the revealed truth, you can explain a part of what it means for a married couple to become one flesh is an act called sex.

This is the most uncomfortable part of the conversation for us adults, but here is a simple way to explain it to your child: "Sex is when a man puts his penis inside of a woman's vagina. This act reminds the husband and wife of the promise they have made to one another: to love one another and stay together for life. God designed sex to help a husband and wife love each other and get to know one another better. Just as shaking hands or signing a contract are acts that seal a promise, sex is the act that God designed to seal the promise of marriage." You can then say to your child, "This idea might sound strange or confusing to you, and that's okay." Remind your child that God designed sex for a husband and wife, and since it will be a long time before your child is old enough to get married, they do not need to understand everything about sex right now.

Similar to the conversation about body parts, you will want to ask your child if they have any questions. Again, if you need more time to think through an appropriate answer, do not hesitate to affirm your child's question and tell them you'll come back to this conversation once you've had some time to think about the answer. To close the conversation, remind your child that sex is something very special that God has designed for husbands and wives to seal the promise of marriage. Sex is so special that your child should not discuss it with their friends or other adults. At this age, they should only talk about it with their parents. If you sense that your child will want to talk about it with their friends, reassure them that their friends' moms and dads will talk about it with them, so your child knows they don't need to be the one to bring it up.

3. TALKING ABOUT REPRODUCTION

The final conversation to start at this early stage is how sex connects to reproduction. I recommend beginning the conversation by taking a walk outside with your child and looking for flowers. After you return home, ask your child if they know how each flower you saw began. You can discuss how each flower began as a tiny seed. Once that seed was planted in the ground, it was watered and received sunlight. All of these elements helped that tiny seed grow into a beautiful flower.

You can then explain that when God created our bodies, he designed them with things similar to seeds. Men are designed with something called sperm. Women are designed with something called eggs. Explain that when a man's sperm meets a woman's egg, a baby begins to grow. You can then say, "We have seen many women who have babies growing inside of them. You may have wondered how the babies got there, and the answer is that they got there through sex. When a man places his penis inside a woman's vagina, his penis releases sperm into the woman's body. When the man's sperm connects with the woman's egg, a baby begins to grow in a special place inside of the woman called the womb. At first the baby is very tiny, but it is kept safe inside of its mother. As the baby grows, the woman's womb stretches bigger and bigger. After the baby grows for about nine months, it is ready to leave the woman's body. God designed the muscles in the mother's womb to push the baby out through her vagina so the baby can be born!"

I also recommend you take your child to Psalm 139:13-14, which says, "You formed my inward parts; you knitted me together in my mother's womb. I praise you, for I am fearfully and wonderfully made." You can then discuss how this verse reveals that all babies are wonderfully made by God. I recommend saying, "God designed sex to lead to babies, and when a baby is growing inside of its mom, God is purposefully designing all the details of the baby—their hair and eye color, what they will be good at, and even what kind of things they will enjoy. All babies are gifts from God!"

Once again, you can ask your child if they have any questions. I also recommend reminding your child that because sex is such a special gift, they should only talk about it with you and your spouse.

If you still feel intimidated by the thought of these conversations, several resources can hold your hand through this process. At Foundation Worldview, we have a three-lesson video series called *"The Talk"…Made Easy*. This series follows the three steps outlined in this chapter and has been designed to introduce the basic terms and concepts to children between the ages of four and seven. Foundation Worldview created these videos for you to watch alongside your child. As your child learns these concepts for the first time, you may then have a follow-up conversation to address any immediate questions they may have.

Another helpful follow-up is the God's Design for Sex series by Stan and Brenna Jones. This series of four books will help you have sex talks with your child at different stages, giving you developmentally appropriate language and illustrations to use as you guide your child. As your child grows, you can also use a series called *The Talk* by Luke Gilkerson. This book contains seven lessons you can go through with your child to cover the biblical basics of sex in a developmentally appropriate way. Each of these resources can support and encourage you as you teach your child about God's good design for sex.

• • •

Talking with your young child about sex need not be complicated or intimidating. With intentionality and proper preparation, you can help your little one understand the basics of God's good design for sex. This will lay the necessary foundation for them to think and live biblically in the future.

3

DOES IT MATTER WHICH PARENT GIVES THE SEX TALK?

One question I often hear parents ask is: "Does it matter which parent introduces the concept of sex?" Should dads have these conversations with their sons? Should moms be the only parents having these talks with their daughters? These are important questions to think through, and I believe the answer depends on the age of our children.

If we start talking with our children about sex when they are very young (around age four), they are not at an age yet where they need to have a conversation with one parent over the other. These foundational conversations can occur with either parent, but ideally, they should happen with both parents. Most young children will not feel embarrassed or awkward having these discussions, and having both parents present teaches children to feel comfortable coming to either parent with their questions about sex.

As children get older, especially after age eight, it is usually beneficial for them to have more in-depth conversations about sex with the parent of the same gender. A mom's perspective on sex and sexuality will likely differ from a dad's, and it can be especially valuable for daughters to learn from their mothers and for sons to learn from their fathers. As these conversations in early adolescence are often tied to puberty, physical development, and personal hygiene, it can be comforting for a child to have these conversations with the parent of their same gender. That parent can best provide wisdom gained from firsthand experience of what his son or her daughter is currently going through. Plus, as children enter the age when talking about sexuality makes them uncomfortable, these conversations can be less awkward when talking with parents of the same gender. While some families may prefer having both parents involved in all of these conversations, as a child grows, it is wise to consider what the child is most comfortable with. Some girls may feel uncomfortable having their dad involved, as may some boys with their mom.

You may be a single parent raising a child of the opposite gender and wondering what you should do. If so, know that God has equipped you for these important conversations with your child. Even though you may feel out of your element, and some of these talks will probably feel uncomfortable in the moment, your child will still benefit from your intentionality in helping them understand the goodness of God's design. More important than the parent's gender is the intentionality and biblical grounding of such talks. As you walk forward in these conversations, you can trust that God will give you the wisdom you need (James 1:5) and use your imperfect efforts for his glory and your child's good (Romans 8:28-29).

If your child's other parent is not in the picture or is not a Christian, it is wise for you to involve other mature Christians of the same gender as your child in your family life. These influences can be grandparents, aunts or uncles, or a married couple from your church. While these individuals are not the ones who should be having the initial sex talks with your child, inviting them into your family life will provide your child with a fuller picture of what it looks like to be a man or woman who faithfully follows Jesus.

• • •

No matter your gender or your child's, you have the important role of introducing them to and grounding them in a biblical understanding of God's good design for sex. And you can rest in the fact that God has both called and equipped you for this role.

4

HOW DO I OVERCOME FEELING EMBARRASSED OR UNPREPARED TO HAVE THESE CONVERSATIONS?

Even after reading through the three previous chapters, you may still feel anxious about talking with your child about sex. You may feel you are in over your head because your parents never had these conversations with you. Maybe your parents *did* talk with you about sex, but the conversations were awkward and you fear making similar mistakes with your child. You may find sex to be something you'd be uncomfortable talking about with *anyone*, let alone your child. Or you may have already had a conversation about sex with your child and felt that it went so poorly you never want to broach this topic again. If this is you, please rest assured that none of these feelings are uncommon! But what should you do to overcome this anxiety?

I think the most important way to overcome these feelings is to remember that God has called and equipped you. God is the One who has entrusted you with your child. And he has given you what you need, in his Word, to ground your child in the truth and prepare them to reject the lies they encounter. Ephesians 6:4 calls parents to bring their children up "in the discipline and instruction of the Lord." Then, just verses later, we are reminded that "we do not wrestle against flesh and blood, but against the rulers, against the authorities, against the cosmic powers over this present darkness, against the spiritual forces of evil in the heavenly places" (Ephesians 6:12). Our culture is overrun by confusion about gender and sexuality, and the spiritual forces of evil would love nothing more than for you to remain silent on the topic of sexuality so your child can become ensnared in culture's lies. Rather than fearing the awkwardness or embarrassment of such conversations, view them for what they truly are: a vital step in grounding your child in the truth and preparing them to reject the lies of the enemy. This understanding should infuse you with the courage to begin these conversations, even if you still feel anxious or embarrassed.

I believe it is also important to recognize where our sense of shame or embarrassment over the topic of sex comes from. In the second chapter of Genesis, after God brought Eve to Adam and united them in marriage, we are told, "The man and his wife were both naked and were not ashamed" (Genesis 2:25). In their perfected state, Adam and Eve felt no shame over their naked-ness—their vulnerability with one another. However, immediately after they rebelled against God by eating from the fruit of the tree of the knowledge of good and evil, "Then the eyes of both were opened, and they knew that they were naked. And they sewed fig leaves together and made themselves loin-cloths" (Genesis 3:7). Sin immediately led to shame over the naked human body. It led to a vulnerability that was no longer safe but was at great risk of harm. It's because we are fallen that we feel shame over sex and sexuality—gifts that God created as inherently good. When we understand where this shame stems from, we will be better equipped to push through this feeling and seek to ground our children in the truth.

Another thing you can do to overcome any feelings of awkwardness or inadequacy is to research and prepare yourself for these conversations ahead of time. The Birds & Bees online video curriculum is a great resource that provides ten video-based lessons, walking parents through different conver-sations about sex to have with their children. The God's Design for Sex series provides four books parents can read with their children at different stages in their child's development. These books provide appropriate vocabulary and clear, concise, biblical answers to many questions about sex. At Foundation

Worldview, our *God's Good Design for Sex* series offers three short videos you can watch with your child to introduce them to the concepts of genitalia, sex, and reproduction. I also recommend *Mama Bear Apologetics Guide to Sexuality and Gender Identity* as a resource for parents who want to understand how to talk about the gender and sexuality messages their school-aged children are receiving from school, peers, and media.

Finally, I encourage you to pray, pray, and pray some more. Pray that God will give you wisdom in these conversations. Pray your words will be clear, in line with Scripture, and honoring to God. Pray that God would soften your child's heart and open their eyes to the beauty of his design. Pray that God would protect your child from pornography, from harm, and from every other form of unbiblical sexuality. Pray that God would help you create an open and trusting relationship with your child, one where your child feels comfortable enough to come to you with all of their questions and concerns. Prayer is essential because God can do what we cannot. We cannot craft perfect sex talks with our children. Neither can we ensure that they will follow God's good design for sex. But we serve a God who loves our children even more than we do. He alone can give us the wisdom we need as we seek to faithfully disciple our children. And he alone can turn our children's hearts toward him.

. . .

Talking with our children about sex may always involve some feelings of anxiety or embarrassment. However, when we remember that God has called and equipped us, acknowledge the root of our shame, prepare ourselves with helpful resources, and cover these conversations with prayer, we can move forward with peace and confidence.

5

WHAT IF I'VE WAITED TOO LONG TO HAVE THE INITIAL SEX TALK?

As you read my recommendation to begin talking with your child about sex around the age of four, you may have thought: *My child is way past four. Is it too late for me to begin the conversation?* And here's the good news: No, it's not too late. Helping your child develop a biblical understanding of sexuality is vital no matter their age. So let's talk through how to have these conversations with older children.

One caveat: When I use the term *older children*, I am referring to children between eight and twelve. Obviously, if you have a child older than twelve, it is still important to begin talking with them about sex. However, my area of expertise is working with children who are twelve and under, so giving advice on talking about sex with a teen is outside my wheelhouse. For parents of teens, I recommend the books *Facing the Facts: The Truth about Sex & You* by Stan and Brenna Jones and *Relationships: 11 Lessons to Give Kids a Greater Understanding of Biblical Sexuality* by Luke and Trisha Gilkerson.

Now, back to the question at hand. My first recommendation for parents of older children is to begin talking about sex *soon*. The longer you wait to start these conversations, the more difficult and uncomfortable they are likely to be when you eventually have them. On top of that, the longer you wait, the more likely your child will have received misinformation that has tainted their understanding of sex. So please do not hold off on these conversations because you are worried you don't have them mapped out perfectly or because you don't feel 100 percent ready to answer your child's questions. For the sake of helping your child understand the goodness of God's design, it is best to have this first talk as soon as possible.

Second, I recommend that you avoid making this first sex talk a big, intimidating moment. You do not need to lay any groundwork by saying something like, "Tomorrow night, we're going to sit down and talk about something really important." Just imagine how fear-inducing it would be if your spouse said, "Tomorrow night, we need to have a conversation about something important." Even if the conversation were about something good, such as a raise or a promotion, you would probably spend the next 24 hours worrying about what terrible news was looming. If you take a similar approach with a sex talk, all of this buildup will make both you and your child feel anxious and uncomfortable—and the result may likely be an even more awkward first conversation (and any follow-up conversations).

Instead, I recommend having more of a casual conversation while you are completing an everyday activity with your child. You could plan to have this first conversation when cooking dinner together, driving your child somewhere, or reading a book together. Bring up the subject in a positive and nonintimidating way. I suggest saying something like, "There's a part of God's good design for humans that I'm excited to talk with you about." You may be thinking, *Elizabeth, no part of me is excited to talk to my child about sex!* To feel this way is understandable, but as parents, it is vital to present sex in a positive way because sex is a positive thing. It *is* a good gift from God, no matter how the world has twisted and abused this gift.

As you begin these conversations with your older child, try to find out what they have already heard about sex. At this age, your child has more than likely already heard the word *sex*, and they've also probably picked up other information (and misinformation!) about sex from conversations with peers at school or even church. So when you have the first talk, you can say, "We're going to talk about a special part of God's good design called *sex*. Have you ever heard that word before?" If they say yes, ask some follow-up questions. I recommend saying something like, "Thanks for letting me know. I'm curious: When have you heard that word?" After hearing their response, you can ask, "So what have you heard about sex?" At this point, you just want to gather information. What do they know? What do they not know? What do they *think* they know but actually *don't* know?

After your child has answered these questions, I recommend thanking them for sharing with you. This response will send a clear message that you are not scared to talk about this topic with them. It also helps them feel you are a safe place to go with their questions. Your child may possibly tell you something they have heard about sex that is off base or completely inaccurate. Even so, you still should praise them for being honest and open with you. And though your instinct may be to explain how what they have learned from their peers is wrong, starting off the conversation with correction will give it a negative spin. Instead, you could say something like, "Thank you so much for being honest with me about the things you have already heard. I'm grateful for this opportunity to talk about sex with you so you can understand what it is and how it fits into God's good design for us."

After that, you can begin talking about the basics of God's good design for sex. I recommend going through the same points I outlined in chapter 2 about genitalia, the mechanics of sex, and reproduction. (Simply take out the examples of toys and flowers that I suggested and stick to the basics.) You might feel anxious or sense that your child is uncomfortable, but no matter how either of you feels, try to stay calm and positive. You will also want to pray before the conversation, asking God to help you stay calm and clearly communicate his good design for sex.

My final recommendation is to consider this talk as an ongoing conversation, not a one-and-done deal. For so long, many parents have viewed "the talk" as a single moment where they sit down with their child, cover the basics, and then look forward to never discussing the topic again. However, developing and maintaining open lines of communication with our children is so important. This means circling back to this conversation, building our children's understanding of God's good design for sex, and asking over and over what they have heard from their peers so we can refute misinformation with the truth.

• • •

It is never too late to begin talking with your children about sex. Even though these conversations may feel uncomfortable, they will help your child gain a clear, biblical understanding of God's good design for sex. They will also build your child's trust, demonstrating to them that you are the safest person to come to with their future questions about sex.

PART 2

TEACHING BIBLICAL VIEWS ON SEXUALITY

6

HOW DO I EXPLAIN SEXUAL SIN TO MY CHILD?

We have already discussed the importance of grounding our children in a biblical understanding of God's good design for sex and marriage. However, we can't stop the conversation there. As humans, we are fallen people living in a fallen world. This means much of what our children encounter in the world around them, and even within their own hearts, will not align with God's good design—so it is important to have conversations with our children about sexual sin. Because these conversations can be both challenging and uncomfortable, you may be tempted to wait to have them until your child is directly confronted with sexual sin in media, literature, relationships, or the community. However, as we have covered in previous chapters, this reactionary approach is unwise. Instead, proactively preparing our children for what they'll encounter is best.

In the following chapters, we'll discuss in detail how to talk with our children about specific deviations from God's good design, such as pornography, masturbation, divorce, homosexuality, transgenderism, and abuse. However, before covering those specific topics, we must simply introduce our children to the idea that not all people follow God's good design of reserving sex for marriage, and any deviation from his design is sin.

The New Testament Greek word for sin is *hamartia*, meaning to miss the mark. This wording is simple enough to explain to your child; sin is missing the mark. An easy way to introduce this concept is to draw a target on a sheet of paper and tape it to the wall. Take an item that is safe to throw inside (such as a squishy ball, bean bag, rubber dart, or small stuffed animal) and stand with your child at the opposite end of the room from the target. You and your child can then take turns trying to hit the target with the object you've chosen. After several attempts, talk about how sometimes you hit the mark, yet other times you failed. Explain how God's perfect law is the mark that all humans should seek to hit. When we miss it, that is called sin. You can then take your child to Romans 3:23, which reads, "For all have sinned and fall short of the glory of God." Discuss how this verse reveals that all humans have missed the mark. We've all failed to live up to God's perfect standard, and this sin separates us from God. Then read Romans 3:24: "[You] are justified by his grace as a gift, through the redemption that is in Christ Jesus." Discuss how God sent Jesus to hit the mark for us. Jesus lived the perfect life we could never live, died on the cross in our place, and rose again to new life (1 Corinthians 15:3-5). Now anyone who turns from their sin and trusts in Jesus is forgiven of their sin and reconciled to God (2 Corinthians 5:17-19).

You can then turn the conversation to sexual sin. Explain that one of the ways humans miss the mark is by not keeping sex within the covenant of marriage. Sometimes people choose to have sex with someone they are not married to. You can take your child to Hebrews 13:4: "Let marriage be held in honor among all, and let the marriage bed be undefiled, for God will judge the sexually immoral and adulterous." Discuss how God has made clear that sex is designed for marriage, and that taking sex outside of marriage is a sin that separates us from God. It is also important to explain that, just like all other sins, taking the good gift of sex outside of marriage is a sin that Jesus died for. Anyone who turns from that sin and trusts in Jesus can be forgiven.

For children eight and up, it can be valuable to help them understand why taking sex outside the confines of marriage is sinful. We will discuss this in more detail in the following chapters. However, a simple way to introduce this concept is to remind your child that sex is the act that seals the promise of marriage (see chapter 2). If the people having sex are not married to each other, their bodies are acting out the promise of marriage. In other words, they are saying, "I am giving all of me to all of you for life," even though they have not entered the covenant of marriage. Among other consequences we will discuss in later chapters, this making and breaking of a false promise leads to much pain and heartache. We are wise to help our children see that God's commands are always for his glory and our good.

• • •

Introducing our children to the concept of sexual sin need not be complicated or overwhelming. When we help them understand the reality of the gospel—that we are sinful and Jesus died and rose to new life to redeem us—we lay the foundation for helping them understand both the goodness of God's design and his plan of redemption.

7

HOW DO I HELP MY CHILD UNDERSTAND WHY SEX IS ONLY FOR MARRIAGE?

I f you grew up in a Christian home, you were probably taught that sex was only for marriage. Your parents might even have followed this message up with a threat as to what would happen if you ever came home pregnant or if they ever found out you were having sex. However, you may not have been given a thorough biblical understanding of why God designed sex solely for marriage, and in this case, you were probably left feeling a bit confused. Maybe you were unsure why reserving sex for marriage was such a big deal. Even if you did end up saving sex for marriage, you may have done so simply to be a rule follower, but you've never been confident about the actual biblical teaching behind this rule.

If this has been your experience, I encourage you to read "Biblical Foundation" at the beginning of the book, where we go into more detail about the biblical teaching on marriage and sex. Then I hope that reading this chapter will give you actionable steps for grounding your child in a biblical understanding of why sex is solely for marriage. If we want our children to embrace God's good design for sex, we must do more than "lay down the law" and follow it up with threats. Instead, we must help them understand the truth, goodness, and beauty of God's design. I believe that doing so involves three distinct steps: 1) link sex to the concept of design, 2) show that God's design is always good, and 3) highlight the practical goodness of reserving sex for marriage.

1. LINK SEX TO THE CONCEPT OF DESIGN

If we link sex to the concept of design, our children will understand that the evidence in the world around us demonstrates that we are not random or accidental but instead purposefully designed. This is the footing our children will need when, one day, sex outside of marriage looks appealing, and they wonder if what we have taught them all of their lives is actually true. Rather than imparting a blind faith that leaves them with little motivation to exercise control of their raging hormones, we want them to see how the evidence around them points to design and, therefore, a Designer who has specific and good plans for them.

To start this conversation, make sure your child understands what design is. In our God's Good Design Curriculum at Foundation Worldview, we define *design* as a purposeful plan. This is a simple definition that even a four-year-old can understand. I recommend you begin by pointing out things in your home that illustrate intentional design. For example, you can point to your child's bicycle and marvel at how the designer made all the parts—wheels, seat, pedals, frame, handlebars—to come together and function as a bicycle. You can ask your child if it is possible that all of these parts came together accidentally to form a bike. Then discuss how this is impossible. Metal, rubber, and plastic pieces do not accidentally come together to form bikes. They must be intentionally designed by *someone*. In fact, anytime you see design, you know the design comes from a *designer*. And the designer of an object understands how that object works better than anyone else because he or she created it. From there, you can take your child to another object around the house and repeat this process. If you make a habit of discussing the design of different items around your home, your child will naturally begin to notice design and how such design always points to a designer.

The next step is connecting this to our bodies. For example, when picking up toys with your child, you can point to your fingers and say, "Isn't it amazing how our fingers can move, bend, and hold things? Our hands show amazing design!" Or, when you are eating a meal, you can say, "Isn't it incredible how our mouths can chew food and our taste buds let us taste so many delicious flavors? Our mouths show such amazing design!" Ask your child if it makes sense to believe this incredible design of our bodies came to be by accident. No!

As you discussed previously, design always comes from a designer. From there, you can talk with your child about how God is our Designer. He came up with an incredible, purposeful plan for how our bodies are supposed to work! This is made clear in Psalm 139:13-14, which says, "For you formed my inward parts; you knitted me together in my mother's womb. I praise you, for I am fearfully and wonderfully made. Wonderful are your works; my soul knows it very well." You can wrap up the conversation by saying, "Just like a bicycle designer knows the design of that bike better than anyone else, God, our Designer, understands our design best!"

The next step is to help your child see that knowing and following the Designer's design is best. For example, the next time your child rides his bike, you can ask, "What if you decided not to follow the designer's design for this bike, and, instead of pushing the pedals with your feet, you decided to use your hands?" Discuss how your child would not be able to travel very far on the bike and might even get hurt in the process. From this discussion, you can help your child draw the conclusion that knowing and following a designer's design is best. And then you can connect this truth to God's design for us. God is our Designer. He understands our design best. Therefore, knowing and following his design is best.

Finally, you will want to connect the concept of design to sex. Remind your child that they have already learned that God is the One who created sex and that his design for sex is good. You can then point out that just as the designer of a bike created certain boundaries for how that bike is to be used (pedaling with feet, not hands), God, our designer, created certain boundaries for sex.

2. SHOW THAT GOD'S DESIGN IS ALWAYS GOOD

The next step in this process is helping our children see that God's design is always good. I recommend taking your child to passages of Scripture such as Genesis 1:31, Psalm 119:68, Psalm 145:9, and James 1:17, all of which talk about the goodness of God and his design. You can read these passages with your child and ask what is revealed about God and his design. Discuss how these passages reveal that God is good and, therefore, his design is good. You can then discuss some of the ways you see the goodness of God's design for us. You can talk about the goodness of God's design for us as individuals—the design of our bodies, emotions, personalities, and giftings. You can also discuss God's design for relationships—the love of family and friends and the wonderful memories created together.

Then connect this to God's design for sex. Say, "Just as God has a good design for our bodies, our minds, and our relationships, God also has a good design for sex." Take your child to Hebrews 13:4, which says, "Let marriage be held in honor among all, and let the marriage bed be undefiled." Then explain, "God's good design is for sex to be enjoyed only between a husband and wife." Remind them that design always comes from a designer and that designers always understand their design best. God designed us. Therefore, he understands our design, including the design for sex, best.

3. HIGHLIGHT THE PRACTICAL GOODNESS OF RESERVING SEX FOR MARRIAGE

Once the foundation of God's design and boundaries for sex has been established, you can begin talking with your child about why these boundaries lead to flourishing and life. If you have already had the different sex talks with your child as outlined in chapter 2, you can remind them that when a husband and a wife have sex within marriage, they get to know one another in a way that no one else has known them. Explain how this is good because it helps them grow close to and love one another. If your child is eight or older, you can explore some of the science behind this. You can explain that two chemicals released in the brain during sex, oxytocin and vasopressin, bond the two people together.[1] Then discuss how amazing it is that God designed chemicals that act like glue to bond husbands and wives, deepening their love for one another.

Next, remind your child that sex leads to the creation of children. You can then explain that marriage is the best place for children because children are usually most secure when they are in a home where both their mom and dad are present.[2] You can then ask your child to list some of the things they love about living with and being cared for by you and your spouse. Discuss how you and your spouse love them, take care of them, play with them, and provide for them in different ways. Then explain that this is another reason why God's design for sex within the boundary of marriage is so good.

Even if you are a single parent, you can cover this topic with your child, as it provides an excellent opportunity to highlight God's loving-kindness. You can explain that even though your family does not look like God's original design of a mom and a dad together in the same home, your hope and prayer is that when your child grows up, they will have a marriage and family that looks like God's good design. You can then tell your child how you have seen God graciously providing for your family physically, spiritually, and emotionally, even though two parents are not present in your home.

* * *

Investing the time in helping your child understand how God designed sex for our good is foundational to helping them see why sex is reserved for the context of marriage. To provide such an understanding is much more valuable than a mere "laying down of the law." When our children understand God's meaningful design, they are much more likely to understand that God's boundaries around sex are ultimately for their own good.

8

HOW CAN I HELP MY CHILD THINK BIBLICALLY ABOUT THEIR BODY?

Teaching our children to think rightly about their bodies is challenging. On the one hand, they will continually be bombarded with images, advertisements, and shows featuring people with ideal and airbrushed bodies. These forms of media subtly teach our children that their value and worth are found in their appearance. On the other hand, the Christian community often treats the body as if it is unimportant and even unspiritual. This attitude can leave our children believing their bodies have no inherent value. To complicate things even further, as our children grow, they will likely endure their own internal struggles with body image. How can we help our children avoid these common pitfalls and train them to see their bodies as God sees them?

I believe that doing so involves three distinct steps: 1) ground our children in a biblical view of their bodies, 2) reinforce biblical truths in everyday situations, and 3) set up healthy guardrails.

1. GROUND OUR CHILDREN IN A BIBLICAL VIEW OF THEIR BODIES

If we want our children to have a biblical understanding of their bodies, we must take them directly to the source: Scripture. I recommend first taking your child to Genesis 2:7, which reads, "Then the LORD God formed the man of dust from the ground and breathed into his nostrils the breath of life, and the man became a living creature." You can ask your child what truths this verse reveals about humans. Then discuss how this verse shows us that humans are both physical and spiritual—body and soul. God created Adam's physical body out of the dust of the ground. Then he breathed Adam's soul, the spiritual part, into him. This means God purposefully created both the physical and spiritual elements of our existence. You can then discuss how God repeated throughout creation that what he'd made was "good" (Genesis 1:4, 10, 12, 18, 21, 25, 31). This means God's design for your child as body and soul is also good.

A helpful follow-up to this verse is Psalm 139:13-14: "For you formed my inward parts; you knitted me together in my mother's womb. I praise you, for I am fearfully and wonderfully made." You can read this passage with your child and ask what truths are revealed about God's design for humans. Then discuss how this passage reveals that God intentionally formed each human while they were still inside their mother. You can talk about how this passage again shows the inherent goodness of God's design for us as body and soul. You can then ask your child, "According to the verses we read, how does God view our bodies?" Talk about how God purposefully designed our bodies, and they are good.

After your child understands that God highly values their body, it is important to introduce how sin has corrupted our bodies as well as our views of them. Genesis 3:6-7 explains this clearly:

> When the woman saw that the tree was good for food, and that it was a delight to the eyes, and that the tree was to be desired to make one wise, she took of its fruit and ate, and she also gave some to her husband who was with her, and he ate. Then the eyes of both were opened, and they knew that they were naked. And they sewed fig leaves together and made themselves loincloths.

You can read this passage with your child and ask what happened right after Adam and Eve rebelled against God. Discuss how they immediately felt shame over their bodies and hid. You can then read Genesis 3:19, which says, "By the sweat of your face you shall eat bread, till you return to the ground, for out of it you were taken; for you are dust, and to dust you shall return." Explain that God is talking with Adam, telling him that because he sinned, he will one day die. You can explain that Adam and Eve's sin led to all humans being sinful (Romans 5:12). Just like Adam and Eve, we experience shame over our bodies, and, just like Adam and Eve, we will one day die. However, this is not the end of the story.

At this point, take your child to Romans 8:23, which says, "We ourselves, who have the firstfruits of the Spirit, groan inwardly as we wait eagerly for adoption as sons, the redemption of our bodies." Discuss how this verse reveals that if we have turned from our sin and trusted in Jesus, our bodies will one day be redeemed. This means they will be made new, restored to how God intended them to be before humans fell into sin. With this understanding of the inherent goodness of our bodies, their corruption by sin, and the redemption offered through Jesus, our children will have a firm footing for understanding a biblical view of their bodies.

2. REINFORCE BIBLICAL TRUTHS IN EVERYDAY SITUATIONS

The next step is to reinforce these biblical truths in how we speak about our children's bodies. We can daily remind our children of the inherent goodness of their bodies by pointing out how amazing the human body is. For example, when your child is at soccer practice, you could say something like, "Wow, isn't it amazing that God has given you legs that carry you so fast down the field and feet that can kick the ball really far?" When your child is putting on their shoes, you could say, "Aren't these five fingers that God has given you on each of your hands amazing? You can tie your laces so quickly with your fingers!" Or, when your child is coloring, say, "Isn't it amazing how all five fingers on your hand work together to hold the crayon so you can make a beautiful picture?" These types of remarks will help frame the way our children think about their bodies.

It is also important to reinforce with our language the times when we see sin's effects on our children's bodies. For example, when your child comes down with a flu or stomach bug, you can say, "Being sick is no fun. These effects of sin on our bodies are not part of God's original design." Or when your child breaks a bone, you could say, "Broken bones are another difficult part of sin's corruption. I can't wait until Jesus returns and our bodies are made new. Then they will never be affected by sickness and injury again!"

As our children enter adolescence and become self-conscious about different parts of their appearance, it will be important to remind them of both the inherent goodness of God's design for their bodies and sin's impact on how we view them. For example, if your adolescent daughter becomes self-conscious about the shape of her nose, you could say, "I know that right now you don't like the shape of your nose, but God designed your nose, and it works well. It allows you to smell, it helps you taste food correctly, and it even helps hold up your sunglasses during the summer. I know you might not want to hear this right now, and you may feel self-conscious or wish you had a different nose. But please remember that all humans experience shame or embarrassment over their bodies. It is never fun to feel this way, but it's the result of sin—and one day Jesus will return, make our bodies new, and remove any shame or embarrassment we may have felt." This type of conversation will not erase your child's self-consciousness, but it will remind them of the truth.

3. SET UP HEALTHY GUARDRAILS

The final step in helping our children develop a biblical view of their bodies is defining healthy boundaries. Our world is full of unrealistic, airbrushed, and filtered images. If we allow our children to spend large quantities of time gazing at or engaging media that pushes unrealistic images, they will begin to think such images are normal, and their body image will naturally suffer. I recommend intentionally reviewing and paying attention to the books, magazines, shows, movies, and video games you allow your child to engage. While keeping your child away from all unrealistic, airbrushed, and filtered images is not possible, you can ensure that most media your child accesses does not contain these images.

As our children grow, it is also important to prohibit them from having social media accounts until at least the final few years of high school. Multiple studies have found a connection between the amount of time adolescents spend on social media and the degree to which they struggle with body image issues.[1] For more information on keeping children off social media, I recommend checking out Screenstrong, an organization dedicated to helping parents make wise technology decisions with their children.[2] Once your child reaches their teen years, I also recommend a course called Refresh Roadmap: A Practical Guide for Parents to Navigate Screen Time & Social Media with Confidence.[3]

. . .

Our children will always face struggles in rightly viewing their bodies. However, by grounding them in the biblical view of their bodies, reinforcing these biblical truths in everyday situations, and setting up healthy guardrails, we can help our children combat false ideas about their bodies and walk forward in the truth.

9

HOW DO I TALK TO MY CHILD ABOUT THE NEGATIVE CONSEQUENCES OF SEX OUTSIDE OF MARRIAGE?

One way to help our children grasp the goodness of God's design for sex is by talking about the practical repercussions of not following that design. Unless children begin asking us questions about this, these conversations don't need to occur when they are very young. Instead, we can wait to have these talks until our children are between the ages of ten and twelve. Postponing these conversations is beneficial because it keeps the consequences from becoming the central focus of sex talks. After all, we don't want our children to obey God simply because they are scared of the repercussions. We want them to live biblically faithful lives out of a love for God. However, once our children are ten and older, these conversations about consequences can help paint a fuller picture of the good boundaries God has placed around sex.

A helpful way to start these conversations is to connect the concept of sexual sin to other ways people can sin with their bodies. For example, we can use our hands for God's glory, but we can also use our hands to sin. With your child, you can brainstorm a list of good things God designed a hand to do: pick things up, carry groceries, scratch our noses, hold a pencil, throw a ball, etc. Then discuss how when we use our hands according to God's good design, we can help ourselves, help others, and do some pretty amazing things. Next, brainstorm a list of ways we can use our hands that go against God's good design: hitting or pushing someone, breaking things, stealing, etc. You can then discuss how when we use our hands in these ways, we end up hurting ourselves and hurting others, and our sin separates us from God.

From there, explain that people can similarly use sex in ways that go against God's good design. Instead of keeping sex between a husband and wife in the covenant of marriage, many people engage in sex outside of marriage. Sometimes people believe God's good design is old-fashioned and keeps them from having fun. But this is not true. God's design is always for our good, and any time we use our bodies in a way that goes against God's design, there are consequences. From here, you can begin discussing four specific types of consequences that result from sex outside the context of marriage: spiritual consequences, emotional consequences, physical consequences, and consequences inflicted on others.

1. SPIRITUAL CONSEQUENCES

While the physical and emotional consequences of different sins vary in degree, the spiritual consequences are always the same: Sin separates us from God. For those who have not turned to Jesus, sin leads to complete separation from God. For Christians, sin leads to hindered fellowship with God. You can take your child to Isaiah 59:1-2, which reads,

> Behold, the LORD's hand is not shortened, that it cannot save,
> or his ear dull, that it cannot hear;
> but your iniquities have made a separation
> between you and your God,
> and your sins have hidden his face from you
> so that he does not hear.

Ask what truths about sin and its consequences are revealed in this passage and discuss how our sin separates us from God. With nuance, explain that for those who have not repented of their sin and turned to Jesus, all sin leads to complete separation from God. When Christians sin, they still have a reconciled relationship with God (Romans 8:1-4), but their sin will hinder their fellowship with God and lead to discipline (Hebrews 12:6). An easy way to explain this is to say, "If you lie to me, you will still be my child. Nothing could change that! But you and I would not be as close as we are now because that lie would come between us. It is the same for Christians. Nothing can stop us from being God's children, but when we do not confess and repent of our sin, that sin makes it so our relationship with God is not as close." To connect this to sex, explain that when we take the good gift of sex outside the marriage covenant, we are sinning against God. This sin continues separating the unbeliever from God and hinders the Christian's fellowship with him.

2. EMOTIONAL CONSEQUENCES

We also want to help our children understand the emotional pain caused when a couple bonds sexually and then breaks that bond. Explain how God made chemicals that are released in a man's brain and a woman's brain during sex. These chemicals act like glue, bonding the man and woman together. When a couple who has sex does not stay together for life, they have been bonded together chemically in a way that makes it much more emotionally difficult to part ways. This does not mean they will be sad forever or that they can never recover from the heartache, but it does mean they will experience more sadness and heartache than they would have had they never bonded through sex. You will then want to circle back to the goodness of God's design, explaining that God designed sex to be reserved solely for marriage so it strengthens the bond between the husband and wife and saves them from the heartache of separation.

3. PHYSICAL CONSEQUENCES

The third type of consequence you will want to discuss is physical consequences—specifically, sexually transmitted diseases (STDs) and sexually transmitted infections (STIs).[1] Be careful not to discuss STDs and STIs to scare your child or manipulate their behavior but instead to help them see the goodness and beauty of the boundaries God has placed around sex. In such discussions, you can explain in very basic terms that people can catch certain infections and diseases, some of which have serious side effects, through having sex. By God's grace, our medical community is developing medications and other treatments to help make the symptoms of these diseases less severe, but some sexually transmitted illnesses never go away. You will then want to briefly discuss some of the consequences of such diseases. Explain that some STIs cause pain during sex. Some cause infertility, making it very difficult for a woman to ever get pregnant. And some more serious STDs weaken the immune system and eventually cause death. Again, we do not want to sit down and have a two-hour conversation aimed at scaring our children out of ever having sex. We just want to provide a basic understanding so they are aware that STDs and STIs exist. Then you can wrap things up by describing how God's design for sex protects us against these illnesses, making clear that if a husband and wife only ever have sex with one another, they will never be exposed to such diseases.

4. CONSEQUENCES INFLICTED ON OTHERS

Finally, we need to address the hurt that can be inflicted upon others. In this conversation, you should talk about the repercussions of children being conceived outside the marriage covenant. You can start this conversation by asking your child to name some of the good things they see about being raised in a home with both a mom and a dad. Emphasize how both parents love the child and seek to care for the child. Then you can talk about how a child knowing that their mom and dad love one another and will always be there for them makes them feel safe. You can also say that no matter whether a baby is born inside or outside of marriage, a baby is always a gift (Psalm 139:13-14; Matthew 19:13-14). But when a child's mom and dad are not married, the child is put in a situation where their mom and dad might not stay together forever. And children who end up living with only one parent usually feel some sense of loss because of their other parent's absence. If you are a single parent navigating these conversations with your child, be honest about the loss you have experienced in your family situation while focusing on how

God has provided for your needs as a single-parent family. Then thank him for this provision.

Finally, it is important to close the conversation by talking about grace and redemption. Our children will encounter many people who choose to reject or ignore God's good design for sex. And, as they grow, some of our children will choose that path as well. We want them to understand that God still extends grace and redemption to sexual sinners (1 Corinthians 6:9-11). This doesn't mean we should brush off the seriousness of sexual sin or make it seem as if those who engage in it will not experience consequences. However, we must make certain our children know that anyone—through repentance—can receive the forgiveness Jesus freely offers through his life, death, and resurrection.

• • •

Talking with our children about the spiritual, emotional, and physical consequences inflicted on others will give them a well-rounded view of the goodness of God's design for keeping sex within marriage. And it will help set the stage for understanding that God's rules always lead to his glory and our good.

10

HOW DO I EXPLAIN DIVORCE TO MY CHILD?

S adly, divorce is a reality in this fallen world, and our children need to understand it from a biblical perspective. However, as we have discussed in previous chapters, we must first ensure we have laid the biblical ground for the inherent goodness of God's design—in this case, God's plan for marriage—before introducing our children to distortions of it.

Most children, simply from observing the world around them, have a basic understanding of what marriage is. And we can build upon this basic understanding by taking them to Scripture and what it reveals about marriage. I recommend first asking your child who our Designer is and what this tells us. If you have already gone through the conversation outlined in chapter 7, your child will know that God designed us, so knowing and following his design is best. You can then explain that God also designed marriage. I recommend taking your child to Genesis 2:22-25, which describes the first marriage God created and is the model repeatedly pointed to in Scripture (Matthew 19:4-6; Ephesians 5:31-33). Read that passage with your child and ask what truths are revealed about marriage.

After your child shares their thoughts, I suggest summarizing the biblical truths this way: "Marriage is one man and one woman becoming one flesh for life." This is a catechizing phrase you and your child can memorize to recall what biblical marriage is. If your child is confused about the term *one flesh*, you can say, "*One flesh* means the husband and wife are working together as a family. They are giving all of themselves to each other." It is key that our children see that God's design for marriage is between one man and one woman—not two men, or two women, or a group of three or more people, but one man and one woman in a covenant with God and each other for life.

Once our children understand the concept of marriage, we can then define divorce as a breaking of God's good design. Divorce happens when one or both spouses decide to break the covenant they made with God and one another. This is not what God originally intended, which is why divorce is almost always incredibly painful for everyone involved.

It is also important to help our children understand that the Bible *does* give permission for divorce in certain cases. For example, directly after affirming the sacredness and permanence of marriage, Jesus makes clear that adultery on the part of one spouse is a justification for divorce (Matthew 19:4-9). In 1 Corinthians, Paul encourages believers with spouses who are not Christians to stay with their spouses. Yet he then writes, "But if the unbelieving partner separates, let it be so. In such cases the brother or sister is not enslaved. God has called you to peace" (1 Corinthians 7:15).

We also want our children to see that not every person who has walked through a divorce is at fault. For example, one spouse may desire to remain faithful to the marriage covenant while the other spouse chooses to leave. But even in these circumstances, divorce is not what God originally intended for marriage, and therefore, the separation is still very painful.

If you and your child's other parent are divorced or are in the process of divorcing, make sure your child understands that the divorce is not their fault. Explain that your divorce is a result of the curse of sin in this world, but it is *not* the result of anything your child has done. Making certain your child knows it is okay and even healthy to grieve a divorce is of vital importance. Feeling sad when God's design is broken reminds us of the gravity of sin's curse. Try not to rush your child through the grieving process, but instead give them time to accept that divorce is a painful thing. However, do not let them wallow in this sadness without any hope; remind them that when Jesus returns, God's good design will last forever. Even though we live in a fallen world where painful things happen, this is not the end of the story. One day, Jesus will return—not as the suffering servant but as the conquering King. He will make all things right, and his good design for us will last forever (Revelation 21:1-5).

If you are reading this while going through a divorce, here are a few other things you can do to support your child:

- Build close relationships with couples and families in your church who have biblical marriages. Even if you are not in a biblical marriage right now, it is important for your child to see biblical marriages modeled for them by other Christians.

- Seek biblical counseling for your child to help them process this divorce. I recommend finding a counselor whose goal will be to work with both you and your child through the grieving process.

- Avoid making your divorce seem as though it is part of God's good design. I have seen well-intentioned friends on social media posting about telling their children things like, "You don't come from a broken home. You come from a home where love has been multiplied." While I understand and sympathize with the desire to avoid shaming children for something they had no control over, children need to understand that the pain they are experiencing is real. Divorce stems from the curse of sin—not God's good design. Then you can lead them to true hope: Jesus has defeated sin, and when he returns, God's good design will last forever.

● ● ●

Divorce is never a fun topic, regardless of whether it directly affects our children. However, if we ground our children in a biblical understanding of marriage, we can explain divorce in a way that helps them understand why it is so painful. Ultimately, this conversation can point them toward the truth of the gospel and the hope we have in Jesus.

11

HOW DO I TALK WITH MY CHILD ABOUT MASTURBATION FROM A BIBLICAL PERSPECTIVE?

Masturbation is probably not a topic you're excited to discuss with your child. However, in our sex-obsessed world, the topic must be covered. You might think this is one conversation you can postpone until your child is in high school. Right? Unfortunately, wrong. You will want to begin this conversation with your child around the age of ten. That's right, ten. Why do I recommend beginning these conversations at such a young age? The sad truth is that many public school curriculums introduce the concept of masturbation around age ten (though some sex education standards recommend introducing the topic as young as eight!).[1] Even if your child is homeschooled or attends private school, he or she will likely encounter the topic of masturbation through a peer at church, at school, or in the community.

Now, before you break into a cold sweat, wondering how on earth you will ever approach this conversation, take a deep breath and remember that God's Word has given you everything you need to live a godly life, including having difficult conversations with your children (2 Peter 1:3). Before discussing how to have such conversations, we must first ensure we have a biblical understanding of the topic. I assume that anyone reading this book has a general understanding of the word *masturbation*. However, just to be safe, let's first define our terms. According to *Merriam-Webster*, masturbation is:

> erotic stimulation especially of one's own genital organs commonly resulting in orgasm and achieved by manual or other bodily contact exclusive of sexual intercourse, by instrumental manipulation, occasionally by sexual fantasies, or by various combinations of these agencies[2]

In short, masturbation is stimulating one's own genitals for the purpose of sexual pleasure. If you are familiar with the Bible, you know God's Word does not directly address the topic of masturbation. There is no "thou shalt not masturbate" command. However, the Bible does have a lot to say about sex, and when we explore the biblical purpose of sex, we can better understand the biblical standpoint on masturbation.

So what is the biblical purpose of sex? We already covered this question in detail at the start of the book. However, a quick review will be helpful as we prepare to think biblically about masturbation. Believe it or not, the Bible begins revealing the purposes of sex right in the first chapter of Genesis. Genesis 1:27 describes God creating humankind in his image. Then, in the very next verse, God explains humankind's purpose and design as his image-bearers by saying, "Be fruitful and multiply and fill the earth and subdue it" (Genesis 1:28). This passage makes clear that one of the biblical purposes of sex is to equip humans to multiply through bringing forth children.

As we continue the biblical narrative, we read that "Adam knew Eve his wife, and she conceived" (Genesis 4:1). The Hebrew word translated here as *knew* is *yadah*. Throughout the Old Testament, *yadah* is consistently translated as *to know* and is used as a euphemism for sex. This euphemism shows that another biblical purpose of sex is for a husband and a wife to know one another intimately. As neuroscientists have learned more about brain chemistry, they have discovered that the chemicals vasopressin and oxytocin, released in the male and female brains during sex, act as bonding agents, developing a strong connection between sexual partners.[3] This chemical bonding further confirms what Scripture reveals: that one of the God-given purposes of sex is to create an intimate connection between a husband and a wife.

A third biblical purpose for sex is revealed in Ephesians 5:31-32, which says, "'Therefore a man shall leave his father and mother and hold fast to his wife, and the two shall become one flesh.' This mystery is profound, and I am saying that it refers to Christ and the church." When viewed within the greater context of Ephesians 5, this passage clarifies that the marriage covenant, including the sexual union between a husband and wife, is a picture of the gospel. As husbands sacrificially lay down their lives for their wives, and as wives sacrificially submit to the loving leadership of their husbands, they paint a picture of Jesus sacrificially laying down his life for his bride and the church joyfully submitting to Jesus's loving leadership. This picture is not limited to the marriage bed, but the "one flesh" union described in Ephesians 5:31 makes clear that sex is included in the symbolism. As such, a third biblical purpose of sex is to paint a living picture of the loving and sacrificial union of Christ and the church.

So when we look at what Scripture teaches about sex, we see three purposes: to be fruitful and multiply, to bond spouses to one another, and to paint a picture of Christ and the church. As we apply this understanding of sex to the topic of masturbation, we need to ask ourselves: Does masturbation fulfill any of the three purposes outlined in Scripture? First, does masturbation lead to the creation of children? No; masturbation is an act of sex with one person. The process of conceiving a child requires a female reproductive system and a male reproductive system. One person, no matter their biological sex, is not physically capable of being fruitful and multiplying. Second, does masturbation fulfill the purpose of spouses getting to know one another? No; whether the person masturbating is single or married, no bonding of spouses takes place in an act of sex that occurs alone. Third, does masturbation accurately paint a picture of Christ and the church? No; masturbation involves only one person. So, rather than painting a picture of Jesus's sacrificial love and the church's loving submission, this act paints a picture of idolatry. In fact, all sex outside of the marriage covenant—whether premarital sex, extramarital sex, heterosexual sex, homosexual sex, or self-stimulated sex—paints a picture of idolatry, of unfaithfulness to Jesus. We can conclude that the Bible does not condone masturbation.

When it comes to having this conversation with your child, you can begin by walking them through the three biblical purposes of sex discussed here and reading them the corresponding passages from Scripture. Then, once they understand this biblical foundation, you can talk with them about what masturbation is. A simple way to explain it is to say that sometimes people touch their private parts in a way those parts should only be touched during sex between a husband and a wife. When people touch their private parts in this way, it usually makes them feel as if they are having sex. This type of touch is called masturbation. You may want to clarify that masturbation is different from when people wipe themselves after using the bathroom or when a doctor examines these body parts to ensure they are healthy. The purpose of masturbation is sexual stimulation. The purpose of those other actions is not stimulation.

You can then explain that masturbation is not a topic you want your child to focus on, but you are talking about it because they will eventually hear about it from their peers, at school, or in the media. So you want to help them to think biblically about it. You can then discuss the reasons described above as to why this act goes against God's good design for sex. When a person is alone, can they be fruitful and multiply by having more children? No. When a person is alone, are they bonding with their spouse? No. When one person is alone, are they painting a picture of Jesus and the church? No. Masturbation does not fulfill any of the biblical purposes of sex. As such, masturbation is not part of God's good design.

. . .

Laying this biblical foundation around the age of ten may not be the most comfortable thing to do. However, by doing so, you are helping your child understand the goodness of God's design and preparing them in advance for the day they are confronted with deviations from it.

12

HOW DO I TALK TO MY CHILD ABOUT PORNOGRAPHY?

ornography is another uncomfortable topic to approach with our children. As Christians, we know pornography is evil. Yet, tragically, pornography is both prevalent and predatory in our society.[1] Today's porn industry is massive, bringing in a minimum of $15 billion per year (though some estimate the true number is closer to a staggering $97 billion).[2] It seeks to draw in and hook our children, thinking only of the dollar signs behind their impressionable hearts and minds and not caring one iota about the severe effects early porn exposure has on children.[3] The prevalence and predatory nature of pornography means we must prepare our children to flee from its evils, regardless of the discomfort that can be involved in these conversations. I know the above information is a lot to take in, but please know there is some good news. The battle is not lost. We can have intentional conversations about pornography that are developmentally appropriate for our children and focus on the goodness of God's design. Such conversations can help them avoid exposure to porn and give them a game plan for when they do encounter it. So now the question is: When do we begin such conversations?

If you have read the previous chapters in this book, I hope you now see the importance of talking with your child about topics related to sexuality before your child is exposed to them. Researchers disagree over the average

age at which children are exposed to pornography. Some claim it is as old as thirteen, while others claim it is as young as eight.[4] I spent a decade teaching at a Christian school, and judging by the number of third graders in my classroom who accidentally encountered porn online or were introduced to it by a friend, I believe eight is a much more accurate age. On top of this, we have grown desensitized to the host of scantily clad magazine covers and advertisements that we (and our children) see every day. But the reality is such images would have been considered soft porn in decades past. For these reasons, I recommend parents have their first conversations about pornography with their children when they are around the age of four. I know this may seem startlingly young, but I hope to model for you how such conversations can be had in a developmentally appropriate way that empowers and protects our children rather than overwhelms them.

As has been mentioned in previous chapters, we always want to start conversations about sexuality by laying a positive biblically sound theology for God's good design before talking about deviations from that design. In this case, first teach your child that all humans bear God's image (Genesis 1:27) and are fearfully and wonderfully made (Psalm 139:14). I recommend taking your child directly to these passages, reading them together, and then asking, "What truths about humans are revealed in these verses?" On a sticky note or index card, you can then write, "All humans bear God's image and are fearfully and wonderfully made." You can post these truths on the fridge, bathroom mirror, or any other place where you and your child will see them daily. These truths are the basis for understanding why pornography is wrong; it takes precious humans, who have been fearfully and wonderfully made in the image of God, and treats them as nothing more than objects of sexual gratification.

The next step is helping our children understand what pornography is. A great way to introduce this concept is by first making sure your child understands *good* pictures. You can travel from room to room in your house and have your child point out the amazing photographs you have hanging on the walls, mounted to the fridge, and placed on shelves. As you look at each picture, point out what is good about each one. "That one reminds us of our amazing camping trip last summer!" "This picture from Grandpa and Gram's wedding reminds us of how much they love us and one another!" "That picture of Cousin Sophie reminds us of how thankful we are for our cousins!" Next, read a favorite picture book with your child. Discuss how the illustrations are also good pictures because they show the characters having fun, being kind to each other, showing courage, or learning a lesson. You can then talk about how there are so many good pictures of people and places you love, as well as illustrations that help you engage with a story.

The next step is to contrast these good pictures with bad ones. At Foundation Worldview, in our God's Good Design Curriculum, we explain pornography by saying, "Because of sin, not all pictures are good pictures." Young kids can memorize this simple sentence to help them understand what pornography is, even if you do not think they are ready to be introduced to the word. (I do recommend that if your child is eight or older, you explain that *pornography* or *porn* are words used to describe this type of bad picture. This way, your child will recognize the words when they hear them.) Next explain that sometimes people take photographs and videos or draw illustrations of others without any clothes covering the special parts of the body that a bathing suit was designed to cover. These pictures are bad because they do not treat the people in the pictures or the people viewing those pictures as fearfully and wonderfully made image-bearers. You can then explain that these bad pictures will sometimes appear unexpectedly in places like phones, tablets, computers, TV commercials, and magazine covers. If your child is eight or older, you can mention that they may have already come across these bad pictures, and you want to help protect their hearts and minds for when they come across such pictures again.

The next step is to give your child a game plan for the moment *when* they see a bad picture. In our God's Good Design Curriculum, we give children a three-step formula: 1) stop, 2) run, 3) tell. Tell your child that when they see a bad picture, they may feel scared inside and want to hide. Or they may feel curious and want to look at the picture longer. But no matter how they feel, the right thing to do is to stop looking at the picture, run to you, and tell you what they saw. Explain that when they do this, you will be so proud of them for doing the right thing. And when they tell you what they saw and where they saw it, that information will help you keep them safe in the future.

If your child is eight or older, you will also want to prepare them for what to do if a friend or peer intentionally exposes them to pornography. Sadly, even when I taught at a school where teachers, administrators, and parents were committed to their Christian faith, this situation occurred numerous times. I recommend teaching your child a simple phrase to help them escape these situations: "Nope, that person is made in God's image. I don't want to look at that picture." A phrase like this not only reminds your child of the inherent worth of the people depicted in the photo, video, or illustration but also helps their friend understand why your child is not going to look at it. It's not because they're scared or a "chicken." It's simply because the people in that picture or video are valuable image-bearers who are not being depicted in that way. Teaching our kids an easy and God-honoring way to say no to porn can give them confidence for the day when they feel pressured by friends to view it.

If you'd like some great resources to incorporate into these conversations, the book *Good Pictures Bad Pictures Jr.* is useful for children ages four to seven. Then the book *Good Pictures Bad Pictures* is appropriate for children ages eight to twelve. The first book helps young children develop a basic understanding of the difference between good pictures and bad (pornographic) pictures. The second dives a bit deeper in a way that is developmentally appropriate for older kids, exploring what occurs in the brain when pornography is viewed and how it rewires the brain in unhealthy ways.

Once you have begun having these vital conversations, your family must also develop habits and practices to intentionally avoid porn culture. For example, if you are watching the Super Bowl and the halftime show is raunchy and suggestive, you obviously don't want to keep watching, but you also don't want to turn it off without saying anything. Instead, turn off the TV and then explain, "The way those people up there are dressed and dancing does not show that they are fearfully and wonderfully made image-bearers. So we're turning this off until the game comes back on."

Installing filtering software on all devices in your household, as well as setting limits around technology use, is also important. For example, devices should be used in your home's common areas and should never be allowed in private spaces such as bedrooms or bathrooms. Even though it may be difficult, parents should model following these boundaries as well, because the same limits will help protect your child from either unintentionally encountering porn or giving in to the temptation of intentionally seeking it out.

Intentional conversations, training, and home habits are great protective measures in the battle against the evils of pornography. However, prayer is another equally vital protective measure. Pray earnestly that God would protect your child from encountering porn online or with friends. Pray also that God would give your child a soft heart toward him, because a heart whose affections are turned toward God is a heart that will recognize pornography for the evil that it is. Pray that if your child does one day seek out pornography, God will convict them of their sin quickly, because a heart that easily recognizes the conviction of the Holy Spirit is one that will not seek to hide sin but bring it into the light. Prayer is crucial in our battle against the evils of pornography.

. . .

The porn industry is predatory, seeking to hook our children. However, we are not powerless in this struggle. With time and intentionality, we can prepare our children with a biblical understanding of why pornography is evil, give them a game plan for the moment they encounter it, establish healthy family habits, and cover our children's hearts and minds in prayer.

13

HOW DO I TALK TO MY CHILD ABOUT WHAT THE BIBLE TEACHES ABOUT HOMOSEXUALITY?

When I was growing up in the nineties, homosexuality was a topic most parents did not feel the need to address with their children. Unless you had a relative or close friend who identified as gay or lesbian, a child could make it all the way through elementary and middle school without encountering a homosexual couple—but today, this is no longer the case. Our children will see depictions of same-sex couples everywhere from the children's section of the public library to seemingly innocuous TV shows like *Arthur* and *Blue's Clues*. And with homosexuality now being both accepted and celebrated in our culture at large, there are few neighborhoods or extended families that do not have neighbors or loved ones who identify as gay, lesbian, or bisexual. This means our children will be exposed to homosexuality much earlier than we were. And because of this, we must prepare our children to think biblically about homosexuality. There are three steps we can take to prepare our children in this way: 1) explain what homosexuality is, 2) explore what God's Word reveals about homosexuality, and 3) discuss how these truths apply to your child. Let's explore each step and how to implement it with our children.

1. EXPLAIN WHAT HOMOSEXUALITY IS

If your child is under the age of eight, the basic idea you want to communicate is that homosexuality takes what God designed to be a relationship between a man and a woman and turns it into one that is same-sex. I recommend you explain homosexuality with the same language we use at Foundation Worldview in our God's Good Design Curriculum. In those materials, we say, "Because of sin, sometimes we desire the wrong kind of love in relationships." We explain that sometimes two men or two women desire to get married. Then we remind the children that God designed marriage to be one man and one woman becoming one flesh for life. So two men or two women desiring to get married does not follow God's good design.

If your child is eight or older, I recommend saying something to the effect of, "Because all humans are born with a sin nature, we often desire things that go against God's good design." Then you can discuss some sinful desires that you and your child experience daily, such as fighting to always get your own way, being impatient, lying, using words that tear others down, being selfish, etc. You can then say, "Just as we have sinful desires in these areas, we can also have sinful sexual and romantic desires. For example, if a wife wanted to go on a date with a man who wasn't her husband, that would be a sinful desire. If a husband wanted to kiss a woman who wasn't his wife, that would be a sinful desire." You can then explain that sometimes people desire to be in a romantic relationship with someone who is the same sex as them. Circle back to how God designed romantic attraction to lead to marriage, and marriage is one man and one woman becoming one flesh for life. Then explain that two men or two women dating one another or marrying one another does not align with God's good design.

If your child is over the age of ten, it is also wise to explain the difference between admiration and same-sex sexual desire. As your child grows, he or she will look up to others of the same sex who are often older and have qualities they admire. This is a natural and healthy part of development, and it is different from same-sex attraction. You can explain this by saying, "As you grow, you might look up to someone and think you'd like to be their friend or that you would like to be talented or funny or good-looking the way they are, but this is different from wanting to date or marry them." You can also explain that some people *will* experience same-sex attraction, just as we all experience desires that go against God's good design. You can then explain that if your child ever experiences such desires, you want them to share this with you so you can help them and offer support and encouragement. Make sure your child knows that no matter the temptations they face, you will always love them—and even more importantly, God will always love them and will always want them to draw near to him.

2. EXPLORE WHAT GOD'S WORD REVEALS ABOUT HOMOSEXUALITY

The next step is taking your child directly to Scripture to see what God has revealed about homosexuality. Doing so will help them see that your views on the topic are neither personal nor subjective but are anchored in the objective truth of Scripture.

If your child is under the age of eight, I recommend you take them to Ephesians 5:31-32, which says, "'Therefore a man shall leave his father and mother and hold fast to his wife, and the two shall become one flesh.' This mystery is profound, and I am saying that it refers to Christ and the church." You can then ask, "Who does this passage say is needed in a marriage?...That's right: one man and one woman. And who does the man represent in the marriage?...That's right. He represents Jesus. And who does the woman represent?...That's right. She represents the church." Then you can discuss how two men cannot make a marriage, and neither can two women. They cannot become one flesh in the way God designed for a husband and wife, and they cannot paint the same picture of Jesus and the church.

If your child is eight or older, I recommend taking them to several key passages in the Bible that talk about homosexuality, mainly Leviticus 18:22, Romans 1:18-27, 1 Corinthians 6:9-11, and 1 Timothy 1:8-11. As you read each passage together, ask, "What truths has God revealed in this passage about same-sex relationships?" You can then discuss how Scripture consistently portrays same-sex sexual relationships as sinful. After this, I recommend taking your child to Genesis 2:18-25 and Ephesians 5:22-33 and asking, "What truths does this passage reveal about God's design for marriage?" You can discuss how God designed marriage to be one man and one woman becoming one flesh, and how that relationship is a living picture of Jesus and the church. Finally, ask your child, "Based on what we have seen in all of these passages, does the Bible support any type of same-sex romantic relationship, whether that be dating someone of the same sex or marrying them?" These passages should make clear the answer is no.

3. DISCUSS HOW THESE TRUTHS APPLY TO YOUR CHILD

The final step is to talk with your child about how these biblical truths apply to your child's life. If your child is under eight, I recommend taking them through a simple three-step process they can implement anytime they encounter homosexuality in media or in real life: 1) recognize this is not God's good design, 2) remind yourself of the truth, and 3) be kind.

For the first step, continue training your child to recognize that two men or two women dating or marrying one another is not God's design. Second, have them practice mentally reciting a simple catechizing phrase to remind themselves of the truth. I recommend teaching them this phrase: "God designed marriage to be one man and one woman becoming one flesh for life. God's design is so good." And finally, you will want to teach your child to interact kindly with anyone they meet, including those engaged in same-sex relationships. If your child is eight or older, I suggest taking them through the same three steps and discussing in further detail what it looks like to be kind. Provide practical examples of how they can love others through being kind, as well as how to love others while speaking difficult truths. For more detail on how to walk through these steps, see chapter 24.

* * *

In this cultural moment, we must prepare even our young children to understand what homosexuality is and what God has to say about it. Though approaching this topic may feel intimidating, it can be done well and in a developmentally appropriate way if we focus on explaining the basics, grounding our children in Scripture, and teaching them to recognize the truth and be kind.

14

HOW DO I TALK TO MY CHILD ABOUT WHAT THE BIBLE TEACHES ABOUT GENDER IDENTITY AND TRANSGENDERISM?

imagine that transgenderism is not a topic you look forward to discussing with your child. Yet the world we live in makes it a necessary conversation to have. Like many Christian parents, you may be wondering, *How am I to help my child understand a biblical view of gender identity and transgenderism when Scripture never directly uses these terms?* That is a great question, and I believe that doing so is simple when we take three specific steps: 1) define the terms, 2) explore what God's Word reveals about our creation as male and female, and 3) identify what we should celebrate and what we should avoid. Let's explore each step and how to implement it with our children.

1. DEFINE THE TERMS

Before we can equip our children to think biblically about gender identity and transgenderism, we as adults must make sure we understand how our culture defines these terms. According to *Merriam-Webster Dictionary*, *gender identity* is:

a person's internal sense of being male, female, some combination
of male and female, or neither male or female[1]

In other words, gender identity is not an objective reality that is predeter-
mined. It is a personal, internal, and subjective identity determined by the
individual. The term *gender identity* is rooted in the works of Simone de Beau-
voir, Judith Butler, and Michel Foucault, who all worked toward the goal of
separating gender from biological sex, basically seeking to destroy the distinctions of the male/female binary. Before their work, Western culture generally
understood that some individuals struggled with feeling their identity didn't
align with their sex, but these three writers are responsible for making main-
stream the idea that each individual internally and subjectively decides which
sex they identify with or even that they don't identify with either.

According to the American Psychological Association,

> Transgender is an umbrella term for persons whose gender identity,
> gender expression or behavior does not conform to that typically
> associated with the sex to which they were assigned at birth.[2]

In other words, *transgender* (or *trans*) describes someone whose subjective
feelings about their gender do not align with the objective truth of their biological sex. This can include how a person dresses, speaks, or interacts, expressing dress, speech, or mannerisms typically associated with a gender that does
not align with their biology.

Once we have a clear understanding of how these terms are currently
defined, we can then begin talking with our children about them. If your child
is under the age of eight, the main point to get across is that our feelings do
not always line up with what is true. I recommend introducing the concept
by using the same language we use at Foundation Worldview in our God's
Good Design Curriculum: "Because of sin, feelings can trick us." Explain
that because we are sinful, our feelings do not always point us toward what
is true. It is helpful to follow this explanation with a discussion about different times feelings have tricked you. For example, you may have felt lonely

and assumed no one wanted to be your friend, but the truth was that many people cared about you. Another example could be a time when you felt the urge to say unkind words to someone, but the truth was you should have spoken encouraging words instead. You can then explain that sometimes people allow their feelings to trick them about whether they are a boy or girl. A boy's body will reveal that he is male, but his feelings may trick him into believing he is female, and vice versa.

If your child is eight or older, I recommend saying something to the effect of, "Sometimes our feelings do not point us to the truth." You can then go through examples like the ones given above, allowing your child to share any stories about times their feelings have tricked them. Then explain how feelings that do not point to truth can include feelings about whether someone is male or female. You can explain that many people believe that how someone feels on the inside reveals the truth about whether they are male or female. Sometimes a person's body may reveal that they are male, but on the inside, they feel female, so they decide they really are female, or vice versa. You can then introduce the term *transgender*, explaining that a person who identifies as transgender or trans is someone who feels their gender should be different from what their body reveals.

2. EXPLORE WHAT GOD'S WORD REVEALS ABOUT OUR CREATION AS MALE AND FEMALE

The next step is grounding our children in a biblical understanding of gender. As I have already mentioned, there are few places where the Bible directly addresses transgenderism. In the Mosaic Law, God forbids his people from crossdressing, stating, "A woman shall not wear a man's garment, nor shall a man put on a woman's cloak, for whoever does these things is an abomination to the LORD your God" (Deuteronomy 22:5). However, outside of this command, Scripture contains little about anything we would categorize today as transgenderism. This is because, in Bible times, this issue was not the widespread cultural concern it has become today; therefore, the people of that time didn't need it to be addressed. But the good news is, although the Bible never mentions the modern terms *gender identity* or *transgenderism*, it does speak very clearly about the order of God's creation and the inherent goodness of God's design for men and women.

If your child is under the age of eight, I recommend you take them to Genesis 1:27, which says, "God created man in his own image, in the image of God he created him; male and female he created them." You can ask, "What truths does this verse reveal about how God created humans?" Then you can discuss how humans have been created in God's image as male or female. A great follow-up question would be: "According to this verse, do humans get to choose whether they are created in God's image or whether they are male or female?" You can then discuss how these design decisions were made by God, the Creator—not us, the creation.

If your child is eight or older, I recommend taking them to several key passages in the Bible that talk about God's intentionality in our creation, mainly Genesis 1:27-28 and Psalm 139:13-16. Read through these passages and discuss how God intentionally designed us in the womb. Therefore, our maleness or femaleness is not accidental. It is a purposeful and inherently good part of God's design. After that, consider taking your child to Matthew 19:3-6, Ephesians 5:22-33, and Titus 2:2-5 to see how God's design for maleness and femaleness plays out in important ways in the family and the church. Discuss how Scripture consistently presents maleness and femaleness as being a beautiful and purposeful part of God's intentional design.

3. IDENTIFY WHAT WE SHOULD CELEBRATE AND WHAT WE SHOULD AVOID

At this point, you will want to help your child see that because their biological sex is inherently good, it should also be embraced and celebrated. Many may automatically think, *Okay, so this means I need to make sure my boys are rough-and-tumble and my girls are quiet and dainty, right?* Well, not exactly. If you have a son who is rough-and-tumble, yes; you can and should celebrate how God designed him. And if you have a son who is quiet and artistic, you can and should celebrate how God designed him. Similarly, if you have a girl who is quiet and dainty, you can and should celebrate how God designed her. And if you have a girl who is bold and athletic, you can and should celebrate how God designed her. The point is that no matter the talents, gifts, and personalities God has given our children, we should affirm the goodness of God's creation of them as distinctly male or female. This can be done through verbal affirmations: "I am so grateful that God has made you a boy who is good at drawing." And it can also be done through spending time together as a family: "God designed you to be a girl who loves soccer. Let's go outside and kick the ball around for a few minutes after we finish up the dishes."

As we affirm the goodness of our children's maleness and femaleness, we will also want to directly address why we are not following what the culture teaches about gender identity and transgenderism. If your child is under the age of eight, I do not believe this needs to be addressed any further than the recommendations given in step 2. If your child is eight or older, you can do this through direct conversations and follow-ups. I recommend saying something like this: "We will come across many people in our world who do not recognize the goodness of God's design for us as male and female. Many people think we humans get to choose whether we are male or female and that anyone who says differently is limiting their freedom. However, we know God is our Designer. He is good, and his design is good. When we reject or ignore God's good design for us, we may feel free, but the truth is we are in bondage. Whenever we encounter someone choosing to reject or ignore God's good design, we should seek to love them and show them the truth about God's great love for them in sending Jesus to rescue them from their sin." You can then revisit these conversations any time you encounter a book, show, or situation that is promoting transgenderism and remind your child of the goodness of God's design and our calling to love others by pointing them to Jesus.

* * *

Transgenderism and gender identity will never be easy topics to cover with our children. However, when we invest time in understanding the cultural definitions of the terms, ground our children in a biblical understanding of God's design, and consistently affirm the goodness of God's design for our children, we can help them think and live biblically in a culture of confusion.

PART 3

ADDRESSING ANXIETIES AND FEARS

15

HOW DO I HANDLE THE FEAR THAT I'LL HAVE THESE CONVERSATIONS THE WRONG WAY?

One factor frequently hindering parents from having sex talks early on with their children is the fear of what will happen if they mess up these conversations. If you are wrestling with this fear, you are not alone. Rest assured that it is wise to enter these conversations with caution. However, please do not allow this worry to stop you from grounding your child in a biblical understanding of sexuality. We should be much more concerned about *not* having these talks than about having them imperfectly.

Overcoming these fears requires asking and answering three questions:

1. What is the healthy, reality-based part of this fear?

2. What is the faulty assumption behind this fear?

3. What truth do I need to remember when facing this fear?

Let's work through these questions together so you can approach these conversations with confidence and peace.

1. WHAT IS THE HEALTHY, REALITY-BASED PART OF THIS FEAR?

When it comes to the thought of discussing sex with your child, a part of your fear is healthy. This comes from the rational recognition that these conversations *can* be had in a way that is not ultimately for God's glory or our children's good. Parents *can* have these conversations foolishly. We can share more information than is age appropriate. We can teach and model standards and attitudes that are not biblically sound. We can unintentionally impart to our children a negative, shame-based, and ultimately unbiblical theology of sex. Just as recognizing the need to drive with extra caution during a downpour helps protect us from car accidents, understanding the potential pitfalls of these conversations should lead us to be wise and intentional about what we plan to share.

2. WHAT IS THE FAULTY ASSUMPTION BEHIND THIS FEAR?

While being wise and intentional is important, many parents take their fear to the extreme, assuming that even if they approach these conversations carefully, they might somehow mess their children up for life. But this is a false assumption. Modern psychology has fed us the lie that all problems in adulthood can be traced back to poor parenting. While we should acknowledge that our parenting *does* impact our children, we also must recognize there is no such thing as perfect parenting or perfect child development on this side of Genesis 3. We are fallen. Our children are fallen. We live in a fallen world. We *will* make mistakes in our parenting. Our children *will* make mistakes of their own. Circumstances beyond our control *will* impact us and our children. And because of God's amazing grace, he *will* use it all—the good and the bad—for his glory and our good. Therefore, we need to release this burden of fear, recognizing that faithfully discipling our children does not require perfection. It requires intentionally relying on God's grace.

3. WHAT TRUTH DO I NEED TO REMEMBER WHEN FACING THIS FEAR?

As you seek to overcome your anxiety over talking with your child about sex, here are two important truths to remember. First, God has promised to give you the wisdom you need. James 1:5 says, "If any of you lacks wisdom, let him ask God, who gives generously to all without reproach, and it will be given him." Before starting these sex talks with your child, ask God to give you wisdom about when to speak and what words to use. Ask for wisdom in responding to your child's questions. Then, when you enter these conversations, trust that God will be faithful to his promise.

The second truth to remember is that God will use these conversations, imperfections and all, for good in your life and in your child's life. Romans 8:28 says, "We know that for those who love God all things work together for good, for those who are called according to his purpose." The amazing thing about this promise is that it is not vague. Romans 8:29 explains how God will do this: "For those whom he foreknew he also predestined to be conformed to the image of his Son, in order that he might be the firstborn among many brothers." God will use these conversations to conform you more into the image of Jesus.

MOVING FORWARD WITH CONFIDENCE

As you embrace these truths, here are other practical ways to build your confidence in having these conversations with your child. First, ground yourself in God's Word to cultivate a robust biblical worldview that includes a biblical view of sexuality. God reveals himself to us through his Word, and the more we meditate on it, the more he illuminates the objective truths of Scripture to us in a fresh and personal way. Second, surround yourself with people and resources to support you in this process. Throughout the New Testament, God describes the church as the body of Christ, and he has placed you in your local church to be part of that body. So get to know those in your local church. Look for parents or grandparents who are already doing these things well with their children and build relationships with them. Learn from them. Ask for their counsel as you seek to faithfully disciple your children.

One last thing to remember: As you continue battling anxiety over what will happen if you mess this up, remember that each of us *will* mess this up because we are human. We will not have the perfect responses all the time. We have no idea the questions our kids will ask or the many situations they will face that we'll need to address. But the great thing is, as a parent, you are with your child every day. So if you handle a situation the wrong way, or if you give an answer that you later realize wasn't quite right, just circle back and say, "Remember when you asked me _____ earlier today, and I said _____? As I've thought about it, I've realized my answer does not line up with what the Bible says. So let's talk more about what the Bible teaches in this area." A response like this can powerfully illustrate for your child that even when you do not have the correct answer right away, you know where you *can* find that answer.

. . .

Talking with our children about sex may always be accompanied by some degree of anxiety. However, through biblically evaluating the different components of our anxiety, we can walk forward with humble confidence that God will give us the wisdom we need and use even our imperfections for good.

16

WILL TALKING WITH MY CHILD ABOUT SEX AT A YOUNG AGE STEAL THEIR INNOCENCE?

When I recommend that parents begin talking about sex with their children around age four, I am frequently asked, "But won't having these conversations at such a young age steal my child's innocence?" That's a fair question. To answer it, we must first define the term *innocence*. Innocence has several meanings in modern English. The two that apply in this situation are "lack of knowledge" and "lack of worldly experience or sophistication."[1] Now let's think through this. Will talking with our children about sex take away their *lack of knowledge* about the subject? Yes. Once we begin these conversations, our children will know sex exists. But will talking with our children about sex take away their *lack of worldly experience or sophistication*? No. Talking about the goodness of God's design for sex does not make our children worldly or experienced. In fact, giving them a positive biblically sound theology of sex protects them from the ways of the world by ensuring they are learning God's ways first.

If this sounds strange to you, consider this question: Do you think your child is better off before they learn about sex? If you do, I want to gently suggest that you reevaluate your current understanding of sex. Because we live in a fallen world where human sinfulness has corrupted many good things, it's easy to view sex as inherently dirty. But it is so important for us to understand that the sexual perversion of our fallen world is not God's original design. As we read the entire biblical narrative, we see that sex (within its God-given boundaries) is a good and beautiful thing. In the opening chapter of Genesis, God commands Adam and Eve: "Be fruitful and multiply and fill the earth and subdue it" (Genesis 1:28). This command, also known as the dominion mandate, instructs Adam and Eve to have children. And what method did God give humans to fulfill this command? Sex. From the first chapter of the Bible, we see that sex is part of God's good design.

We see this theme echoed throughout Scripture. Proverbs 5:18-19 says, "Let your fountain be blessed, and rejoice in the wife of your youth, a lovely deer, a graceful doe. Let her breasts fill you at all times with delight; be intoxicated always in her love." Almost the entire book of Song of Solomon describes a bridegroom and bride delighting in their physical love. In the seventh chapter of this love poem, the husband declares, "How beautiful and pleasant you are, O loved one, with all your delights! Your stature is like a palm tree, and your breasts are like its clusters. I say I will climb the palm tree and lay hold of its fruit" (Song of Solomon 7:6-8). Throughout the New Testament, the goodness of sex within marriage is seen in the many commands instructing husbands and wives to be sexually faithful (Matthew 5:27-28; 1 Corinthians 6:18-20; Hebrews 13:4). And in 1 Corinthians 7:5, Paul says that a husband and wife are not to deprive one another of their conjugal rights, except for brief seasons of fasting from sex to devote oneself to prayer. In short, sex within marriage is a good gift that should be enjoyed. Therefore, if we are viewing sex as something inherently dirty or twisted, we need to change our mindset.

Living in a culture of rampant sexual perversion makes it challenging to view sex through the biblical lens. The messages we receive every day in advertisements, social media posts, movies, shows, and, sadly, even from some Christian friends, tempt us to conform to the world's view of sex. On top of this, your experience with sexual sin—whether your own sin or sin committed against you—can make it incredibly difficult to believe what God has revealed about the goodness of sex. (If you are struggling with past sexual sin or sexual abuse or trauma, I highly encourage you to seek out biblical counseling through your church to begin or continue the journey toward healing.)[2] However, as with every other area of life, our responsibility as followers of Christ is to know, believe, and obey what God has revealed in his Word. We are to strive daily not to conform to the pattern of this world but to be transformed by the renewing of our minds (Romans 12:2). And God's Word is clear that God's design for sex is inherently good.

When we have a biblical understanding of sex, I hope it becomes clear that our children are not somehow better off before they learn about it. However, you may still wonder, *Will giving my child knowledge of sex make them start thinking about it years ahead of when they otherwise would?* The answer to this question is yes and no. Yes, talking with our children about sex at an early age will make them conscious of sex before they otherwise would have been (at the age they would've naturally been introduced to the topic by a friend, media, a sex-ed lesson at school, or an accidental encounter with pornography). However, the answer is also no because introducing the topic of sex at an early age will not cause our children to start obsessing over the topic. Unless a child has been a victim of sexual abuse or has been exposed to pornography, he or she will likely not begin visualizing what the act of sex involves. They might have some questions, but their young curiosity is mostly abstract.

If your child struggles with obsessive tendencies, and you suspect they may spend too much time thinking about what the act of sex actually looks like, you can get ahead of this by addressing it in one of your initial talks. You can say, "I really appreciate how curious you are about God's good design for sex. But we are not going to let our minds dwell on what this looks like or how this happens. When you begin to wonder about it, remind yourself that sex is only for marriage—which means you do not need to think about it right now. Then think about another good part of God's design instead, like how he created your legs to run really fast or how he designed your mouth to taste delicious food." If they later ask you "What does this look like?" or "How does this happen?" you can encourage them to ask questions about a different part of God's good design (that isn't related to sex) instead. However, most kids won't follow this line of thinking on their own.

• • •

Once we grasp the inherent goodness of sex within marriage, it should become clear that knowledge of sex, as God designed it, does not steal our children's innocence. Rather, it protects it. By talking with our children about sex at an early age, we ensure they are grounded in God's ways before they encounter any deviations from his good design.

17

HOW DO I DISCUSS SEXUAL PURITY WITHOUT MAKING MY CHILD FEEL SHAME OR GUILT?

You have probably noticed that the concept of "sexual purity" has recently received a lot of backlash from Christians and non-Christians alike. Many of those who grew up in what is now dubbed the "purity culture" of the 1990s and early 2000s say the teachings they received were harmful and induced unnecessary guilt and shame. While we do not have time in this chapter to explore the different ways purity culture did or did not miss the mark, I believe we ought to have a biblically grounded understanding of sexual purity so we do not burden our children with unbiblical guilt or shame as they seek to honor God with their sexuality.

As I sat down to write this chapter, I began thinking about my own life. I am currently in my late thirties and still single. As I have dated over the past two decades, one of the ways I have sought to honor God in such relationships is by setting clear physical boundaries. And, though it may cause you to chuckle a bit, the truth is I have never allowed any of the men I've dated to kiss me. Because we tend to define purity as a lack of sexual experience, I know many people would look at this area of my life and say, "My goodness, Elizabeth, you certainly are sexually pure." However, from the biblical perspective, this is not true. There is no such thing as purity on our own merit. None of us is pure before God.

Romans 3:10-12 speaks to this, saying, "None is righteous, no, not one; no one understands; no one seeks for God. All have turned aside; together they have become worthless; no one does good, not even one." This passage reveals that none of us is pure, sexually or generally. David echoes this truth in Psalm 51:3-5 by saying,

> I know my transgressions, and my sin is ever before me. Against
> you, you only, have I sinned and done what is evil in your sight,
> so that you may be justified in your words and blameless in your
> judgment. Behold, I was brought forth in iniquity, and in sin did
> my mother conceive me.

This passage makes clear that each of us has failed to uphold God's perfect moral law. Not only do we actively choose to sin against God, but also we are sinful from conception, having inherited the sin of Adam. We do not enter this world as blank slates. We enter it as image-bearers of the Holy God who have been corrupted by sin. This means we cannot truly be sexually pure outside of the righteousness purchased for us by the precious blood of Jesus (2 Corinthians 5:21).

Rather than talking with our children about sexual purity, let's reframe this conversation as "sexual faithfulness." Sexual faithfulness is striving to obey God's commands by relying on his grace and turning to him for forgiveness when we fail. Now, I am not suggesting we focus on God's grace in a way that undermines the seriousness of sexual sin and its consequences. Ephesians 5:3-6 and 1 Corinthians 6:9-11 make clear that sexual sin should not be taken lightly, and our children should know that while Jesus's blood cleanses us from all unrighteousness, it does not take away the earthly consequences of sexual sin. (You can read more about this in chapter 9.) However, when we recognize that we are not capable of sexual purity on our own, we can be honest with our children about the reality of sexual sin without burdening them with unbiblical guilt or shame. Yes, when we sin, we rightly experience guilt and shame; but when we turn to Jesus in confession and repentance, we are washed clean and can walk forward in Jesus's perfect righteousness.

I believe that talking with our children about sexual faithfulness involves introducing them to four different truths:

TRUTH 1: SIN CORRUPTS GOD'S GOOD DESIGN

We can take our children to Romans 5:12, which states, "Sin came into the world through one man, and death through sin, and so death spread to all men because all sinned." We can then discuss how Adam's sin spread to all people and corrupted God's good design. If your child is under eight, you can explain the word *corrupt* by saying it is a fancy word that means to ruin or destroy. Because Adam and Eve chose to rebel against God, we have inherited their sin. This means we are born sinful, and this sin has corrupted God's good design.

TRUTH 2: JESUS DEFEATED THE POWER AND THE PUNISHMENT OF SIN

Next we can take our children to Romans 5:6-8, which reads, "For while we were still weak, at the right time Christ died for the ungodly. For one will scarcely die for a righteous person—though perhaps for a good person one would dare even to die—but God shows his love for us in that while we were still sinners, Christ died for us." We can then discuss how Jesus defeated the power and punishment of sin through his life, death, and resurrection. This means that those who have turned from their sin and trusted in Jesus are now empowered by the Holy Spirit to follow God's perfect law.

TRUTH 3: BECAUSE OF SIN, WE OFTEN REJECT OR IGNORE GOD'S GOOD DESIGN

As we rejoice in the freedom Christ has purchased for us, we also want our children to understand that even as Christians, we will be tempted to sin. A great scripture to help our children understand this is Isaiah 53:6, which says, "All we like sheep have gone astray; we have turned—every one—to his own way; and the LORD has laid on him the iniquity of us all." We can discuss how, like wayward sheep, we will continually be tempted to stray. But when we give in to that temptation, the proper response is to confess and repent of our sin, to receive Jesus's forgiveness, and by the power of the Holy Spirit, to walk forward in obedience.

TRUTH 4: WHEN JESUS RETURNS, GOD'S GOOD DESIGN FOR US WILL LAST FOREVER

Finally, we want to help our children understand that our current experience on this earth is not the end of the story. When Jesus returns, he will get rid of sin and death forever. And if we have turned from our sin and trusted in Jesus, we will live forever in the new heaven and new earth. We can take our children to Revelation 21:3-4, which says,

> I heard a loud voice from the throne saying, "Behold, the dwelling place of God is with man. He will dwell with them, and they will be his people, and God himself will be with them as their God. He will wipe away every tear from their eyes, and death shall be no more, neither shall there be mourning, nor crying, nor pain anymore, for the former things have passed away."

Then we can discuss how corruption from sin will be no more in the new heaven and new earth. God's good design for us will last forever!

We want our children to understand that we *all* will struggle with sin, including sexual sin. As painful as acknowledging it may be, our children *will* sin sexually at some point in their lives, whether by entering a sexual relationship before marriage, viewing pornography, lusting after someone, laughing at raunchy jokes, dressing in a way that purposefully attracts sexual attention, or taking part in other sexual sins. We will all fall short of the perfect standard of purity Christ has set for us—and we must turn to God to receive his forgiveness, his grace, and the power to walk forward in faithfulness.

• • •

Ultimately, when we reframe the conversation from one of sexual purity to one of sexual faithfulness, we set up a paradigm that makes it easier for children to understand the goodness of God's design, the great love he has for them, and their absolute need for Jesus's salvation, redemption, and sanctification.

18

HOW DO I HELP MY CHILD NOT BUY INTO THE LIE THAT THE BIBLE'S TEACHING ON SEXUAL MORALITY IS OPPRESSIVE AND EVIL?

When I was a teen in the early 2000s, most of my friends in my public high school thought it was "weird" that I believed sex was reserved for marriage. When my sister entered high school a mere six years later, her friends had similar thoughts about her views on sex, but now they also thought she was weird for believing homosexuality was sinful. Fast-forward two decades, and belief in the biblical sexual ethic is no longer considered merely weird; it is considered oppressive and evil. Why has such a drastic shift in public opinion taken place? And how can we help our children combat this lie they will encounter at every turn? First we will explore the *why* and then look at the *how*.

Understanding *why* our culture's views on gender and sexuality have so drastically shifted over the past two decades is a long and complicated conversation. For a thorough treatment of the topic, I highly recommend Carl Trueman's book *Strange New World*. However, the very, very, very basic answer to the question lies in two little words: *personal autonomy*. You've probably heard the phrase "you do you" thrown around by men and women, adults and children, Christians and non-Christians alike. The phrase encapsulates well the spirit of our age. Our secular culture views personal autonomy—the removal of any and all boundaries and limitations—as the ultimate good. Have you noticed how this message is preached in media? "Follow your heart" is a maxim present in almost every movie and streaming series. In Disney's *Frozen*, Elsa sings this anthem in *Let It Go*, claiming she is beyond rules and is, therefore, truly free. If personal autonomy is the ultimate good, what naturally becomes the ultimate evil? Boundaries and limitations. Because the Bible places boundaries and limitations around sexual expression, the Bible—along with anyone who believes what the Bible teaches—is viewed as evil and oppressive. So now we find ourselves in a world that not only scoffs at the biblical sexual ethic but also seeks to eradicate it.

So *how* can we help our children recognize this line of thinking as false in a world that aggressively promotes it? While this may seem like a daunting question, the good news is we have reality on our side! Looking at the world around us, we see many areas where boundaries are necessary and good. For example, you probably allow your child to play in many places—your backyard, the playground, the park, the pool, etc. However, you do not allow them to play in the middle of a crowded parking lot. You have set this boundary because a quick game played in the middle of a parking lot puts your child at great risk of being run over by a car. Similarly, we subject ourselves to limits as adults because we know they are good for us and those around us—such as driving painfully slowly in a school zone, taking only the prescribed amount of pain medication, eating no more than one scoop (or three) of ice cream, and keeping metal dishes out of the microwave. These and countless other limits hinder our personal autonomy, yet they ultimately lead to our health, safety, and flourishing. And the same thing could be said of the limits God has placed around sex; they lead to health, safety, and flourishing.

Just think about it. What would happen if everyone actually followed the biblical sexual ethic? What would the world be like if we stopped lusting after one another and instead viewed every human as an image-bearer of the holy God (Matthew 5:28; 1 Timothy 5:1-2)? What would happen if every person reserved sex solely for marriage (Exodus 20:14; Hebrews 13:4)? What would happen if every husband loved his wife sacrificially in all areas, including the bedroom, and all wives respected and submitted to their husbands (Ephesians 5:22-33)? What would happen if husbands and wives regularly engaged in sex, fasting from it only for short periods of seeking God through prayer (1 Corinthians 7:3-5)? Can you imagine what the world would be like?! No more pregnancies outside of marriage, no more abortions, no more sexually transmitted diseases, no more sexual abuse, no more rape, and no more sexually starved marriages. Is this vision of the world one of oppression and suffering? No, it is one of true freedom and flourishing! This is what we want our children to see.

A simple object lesson to demonstrate this for your child involves playing a favorite family board game. Play one round of the game according to the set rules. Throughout the round, mention how much fun the game is. Then play a second round, but do not follow any of the rules. Roll the dice whenever you feel like it, not just on your turn. Move your piece at will, no matter what number you rolled. Take as many cards, resources, or pretend dollars as you desire. Every time your child protests, simply say, "Rules just limit my freedom. I'm going to play without any limits this round." Once your child exhibits some frustration, stop the game to debrief. Discuss how the rules of the game do limit what you can do. They take away some of your autonomy. But then talk about the chaos that ensues when you get rid of these rules. You cannot play the game without rules, and you wouldn't want to either!

Then connect this experience to what the Bible teaches about sex. Discuss how God has placed boundaries around sex. Ask your child if he or she can remember some of those boundaries. Then discuss how many people do not like these boundaries. They believe there shouldn't be any limits to who, when, and how they can have sex. Explain that when sex is taken outside of a one-man-and-one-woman marriage, pain, hurt, and chaos ensue. (For a thorough explanation of talking to your child about the consequences of sex outside of marriage, see chapter 9.) Then you can say, "Just as the designer of this game created rules to help us best enjoy this game, God, our Designer, gave us rules for how sex should be used so we can best enjoy it and stay safe from the consequences of sex outside of marriage."

• • •

As your child grows, you should come back to this conversation again and again. We live in a world that seeks to conform us to its values and beliefs. If we are not diligent at renewing our minds in the truth (Romans 12:2), we and our children will easily be taken captive by this errant way of thinking. Press on, friend—reminding yourself and your child that every boundary God has placed on sex is ultimately for his glory and our good.

19

HOW DO I HELP MY CHILD UNDERSTAND THAT FEELINGS DON'T DICTATE SEXUAL MORALITY?

Have you ever watched a movie or TV series and suddenly found yourself cheering for a sinful relationship? The first time this happened to me, I was sixteen and at a friend's sleepover. I don't remember what movie we were watching, but I know one of the main characters was married and eventually left their spouse to be with the other main character. I felt thrilled about this relationship—the exact emotion the movie was designed to elicit—when suddenly, I realized I had just rejoiced over the sin of adultery! How had this happened? Something similar occurred almost a decade later when one of my roommates invited me to watch a new TV series with her. Two episodes in, I decided this series was not for me, as one of the main characters was pursuing a same-sex relationship, and I found myself wanting it to work out. Once again, I was rejoicing over something God calls sin! These two situations highlight one of our culture's main lies about sexuality: My feelings about a relationship determine whether it is right or wrong.

Our children will face this lie at almost every juncture—in books, movies, shows, the classroom, the playground, and even their own hearts. This lie is challenging to combat because rarely is it blatantly stated, yet it is assumed everywhere. As your child grows, they will likely hear this lie in the form of slogans such as "love is love," or emotional claims such as "this is just the way I am" or "I can't help myself." If we are honest, this lie is one we often find bubbling up in our hearts when our emotions become strong or heated. So how can we prepare our children to encounter this lie both from outside influences and from within? I believe doing so involves two steps: 1) discerning objective truths from subjective emotions and 2) identifying when emotions point toward the truth and when they point away from it.

1. DISCERNING OBJECTIVE TRUTHS FROM SUBJECTIVE EMOTIONS

Helping our children understand the difference between objective truths (truths outside the control of our inner emotional world) and subjective emotions is vital. An easy way to introduce this concept is to play a "truth or feelings" game. For this game, explain that you will give your child a statement. They will then need to figure out if the truth of that sentence is *outside* the control of their feelings or *under* the control of their feelings. If your child is seven or younger, you can attach hand motions to truths (arms spread out) and feelings (arms hugging self) so their bodies are also involved in the game. Next, think of different sentences for your child to evaluate. For example, you could say, "Puppies are baby dogs." This sentence is objectively true. No one's emotions can change it. I could believe with my whole heart that a golden retriever puppy is a baby woolly mammoth, but my feelings could not change the truth that this puppy will grow into an adult dog. Then you could say, "Puppies are fun." This sentence represents someone's subjective feelings. Many people feel that puppies are fun. However, others may be allergic to dogs or think puppies are too much work, so for those people, puppies do *not* feel fun. Unlike objective truths, subjective feelings change from person to person.

After playing several rounds of this game, you can add moral claims about things that are right or wrong. Say something like, "It is wrong to hurt others for fun." This sentence is true. No matter how much someone may enjoy hurting others, their feelings do not change the truth that hurting others for fun is wrong. You can then add a sentence relating to sexuality, such as, "God designed sex for marriage." This sentence is also true. If God is real and he has revealed what's right and wrong in the Bible, then our feelings cannot change this statement.

You can begin playing this game in the car or while you are waiting in line at the store. The more you play it with your child, the more you will solidify in their mind these categories of objective truths and subjective emotions.

2. IDENTIFYING WHEN EMOTIONS POINT TOWARD THE TRUTH AND WHEN THEY POINT AWAY FROM IT

Once you have helped your child differentiate between truths and feelings, the next step is to help them discern when emotions point toward the truth and when emotions point away from it. This step is important because, without it, our children will easily buy into another lie: that emotions are bad and should be ignored or stuffed down. This simply is not true. Emotions are not bad. God designed us with emotions, so they are inherently good. However, as with every other part of us, our emotions have been affected by the fall (Genesis 3). Therefore, we must discern when our emotions point us to the truth and when they deceive us.

An easy way to start this conversation is to simply tell your child: "Sometimes feelings point us to the truth, and sometimes they trick us." You can then play a game where you give your child sample situations (real or fabricated) where someone feels something, and your child needs to determine if that feeling is pointing them to the truth or away from it. For example, you could say, "When I was growing up, my little brother took my favorite toy without asking. I felt angry that he used that toy without my permission, and I felt like the best thing for me to do was hit him. Was my feeling of anger pointing me toward the truth or away from it?" In this situation, the emotion of anger tricked you into believing you should hurt your brother. Or you could say, "When Grandma was a little girl, she didn't like school because her teachers always yelled at her and she felt sad. So she decided to become a teacher when she grew up so she could be kind to students and help them. Did Grandma's feeling of sadness point her toward the truth or away from it?" In this situation, the feeling of sadness pointed Grandma to the truth that she should seek to treat others kindly.

You can help solidify this concept in real-life situations when your child experiences strong emotions. For example, if your child experiences frustration and manages that feeling in a positive way, affirm how well they did in not allowing their frustration to trick them. Or, if your child experiences anger and does not manage it positively, at a later time (once their emotions have cooled) you can help them debrief by asking whether their anger pointed them toward the truth or away from it. If you are interested in more games and activities to solidify these concepts, I highly recommend checking out our Biblical Worldview and Comparative Worldview curricula at Foundation Worldview. In both curricula, the entire first unit focuses on truths, emotions, and helping children discern the difference between the two.

Once you have grounded your child in these two concepts, you can begin applying them to everyday life. For example, when you are watching a show and the character says something to the effect of "I need to follow my heart" or "I need to be true to myself," you can ask your child whether the character is following the truth or following their emotions. The exciting thing about this process is that children under the age of ten pick this up quickly.

Not long ago, a mom emailed us at Foundation Worldview to share how our Biblical Worldview lessons on truth had prepared her daughter to think biblically in a situation the mom hadn't expected. One day, this mom's first-grade daughter came home from school and said she'd had a substitute teacher at school that day, a man wearing a dress and going by the name Mrs. So-and-So. The mom had not yet had a conversation with her daughter about transgenderism and immediately began to panic. However, she took a deep breath and asked her daughter what she thought about the situation. Her daughter replied, "Mommy, it was so sad. The truth is that God created him as a boy. But instead of believing the truth, he let his feelings trick him." This is the type of discernment we want our children to develop as they continually face the claim that emotions are the best guide to morality.

• • •

Our children will constantly face the lie that sexual morality is rooted in their feelings. However, once we train them to discern the difference between objective truths and subjective emotions, they will have the skills they need to determine when an emotion is pointing them toward the truth and when it is deceiving them.

20

AM I HYPOCRITICAL IF I TEACH MY CHILD THE BIBLICAL DESIGN FOR SEX, EVEN THOUGH I DID NOT FOLLOW IT?

As you begin the journey of talking with your child about God's good design for sexuality, you may now be experiencing guilt and shame over your past sexual sin. In fact, you may be wondering, *Should I just avoid these conversations? Wouldn't it be hypocritical to teach my child the biblical view of sexuality when I did not follow it?* If you are asking these questions, you are not alone. On the *Foundation Worldview Podcast*, numerous parents write in every year asking these questions, so it is an important topic for us to think through biblically.

If you are in this position, the first question to ask yourself is: *Have I repented of my past sexual sin?* Whether you engaged in sexual relationships before marriage or struggled with pornography, masturbation, or another form of sexual sin, Jesus bled and died so you might be forgiven. If you have already repented of your sin, you have been washed clean. This means any guilt or shame you are experiencing is not from God.

Romans 8:1 boldly states, "There is therefore now *no condemnation* for those who are in Christ Jesus" (emphasis added). Then, in 1 Corinthians 6:11, after the apostle Paul describes a host of egregious sins (many of them sexual in nature), he writes, "Such were some of you. But you were washed, you were sanctified, you were justified in the name of the Lord Jesus Christ and by the Spirit of our God." So if you are in Christ, you are no longer condemned. If you have repented of your past sexual sin, you have been washed clean.

However, you may be in a place where you have not yet repented of past sexual sin, or your past sexual sin may also have become a present and habitual sin. If this is the case, the conviction you are experiencing is the Holy Spirit graciously calling you to repent and receive God's forgiveness. God promised his children that "If we confess our sins, he is faithful and just to forgive us our sins and to cleanse us from all unrighteousness" (1 John 1:9). If you have been walking in habitual sexual sin and have not found victory over it, I encourage you to confess this sin to a trusted believer of the same gender, someone who is more mature in the faith and can guide you and hold you accountable. James 5:16 says, "Therefore, confess your sins to one another and pray for one another, that you may be healed. The prayer of a righteous person has great power as it is working." Depending on the severity of your sin, you may also want to confess it to the elders at your church so they can faithfully fulfill the role of shepherding you (Hebrews 13:17).

Once you have repented of your sin and received God's forgiveness, the question still stands: Are you being hypocritical if you teach your child God's design for sex when you have not followed it? To answer that question, we need to think through what it means to be hypocritical. According to *Merriam-Webster*, hypocrisy is "feigning to be what one is not."[1] This definition should make clear the difference between hypocrisy and integrity. Hypocrisy would be to teach one thing to your child, acting as if you are perfectly living out that teaching, while secretly doing just the opposite. Integrity is teaching the truth to your child, being honest about where you have failed, and, by God's grace, walking forward in faithfulness.

So what does this look like in practice? I believe it involves three steps. First, we need to instruct our children in the basics of God's good design. Before talking with our children about our own sexual failings, they need to know what God's design for sex is. (For more on how to have this conversation, see chapter 2.) Second, we need to frame God's design within the context of the gospel, talking with our children about sin, grace, and sexual faithfulness. Our children need to understand that we are incapable of perfectly obeying God's law on our own. None of us stands righteous before God on our own merit; only through being clothed in the righteousness of Christ and empowered by the Holy Spirit can we live sexually faithful lives. (For more on talking with our children about sexual faithfulness, see chapter 17.) Finally, we must be honest and admit we have not followed God's design perfectly. We must explain that we have sinned sexually and have walked through the natural consequences of our sin. Yet, because of God's amazing grace, we have been forgiven through Jesus's life, death, and resurrection.

• • •

If you have repented of your sexual sin and are walking forward in the grace of God's forgiveness, please do not buy into the lie that you are being a hypocrite by teaching your child about God's good design for sexuality. This is nothing more than a scare tactic of the enemy to silence you from instructing your child in the truth. God has called you and equipped you, and your story of repentance, grace, and redemption will only further highlight for your child the goodness of God and his design.

21

HOW HONEST SHOULD I BE WITH MY CHILD ABOUT MY PAST SEXUAL SIN?

How honest you should be with your child about your past sexual sin is a tricky topic. Speaking to them as if you followed God's good design for sex when you did not would be lying, but giving them a full account of your sexual history would be inappropriate. So what is a healthy balance of walking forward with honesty and integrity without oversharing? I believe such conversations involve three different areas of wisdom: timing, details, and focus.

1. TIMING

I recommend waiting to volunteer information about your sexual sin until your child is ten or older. By this time, your child may be developing crushes or romantic interests, and you will want to be honest with them that following God's good design will not be easy. This is when you can share the struggles you had with sexual sin. Sharing your struggles can help strengthen your relationship with your child at a time when he or she may begin pulling away. I saw this happen in my own life. Though my mom was never ensnared in sexual sin, when she openly shared about her different struggles during her childhood and teen years, it made me more comfortable going to her with my own struggles. Similarly, opening up in an appropriate way once your child is ten or older should make it easier for them to come to you with their struggles.

As a side note, even if you do not bring up this conversation until your child is ten, your child may still ask you questions about your sexual past before they reach that age. In such cases, it is okay to be honest and tell your child you did not follow God's good design—yet you will want to ensure you are not going into more detail than is necessary and appropriate. This brings us to the next area in which wisdom is needed: details.

2. DETAILS

I recommend only sharing general details of your past sin, because going into specifics would not be helpful for your child to hear or for you to relive. For example, if you engaged in sexual relationships before marriage, you could say something vague, such as: "In college, I dated a few different guys. Rather than following God's good design, I chose to have sex with them. That was sin." Or, if you have struggled with a pornography addiction, you could say, "When I was in middle school, I stumbled across pornography. After that, I kept watching more and more until it became a sinful habit that I felt I couldn't break free from." If you feel it is appropriate, share a detail or two about the consequences you faced from this sexual sin.

Though many forms of sexual sin involve another person, it is not wise to share details that would reveal the identities of any other people. To do so would not be respectful to the other person who did not give you permission to share this information, and it would not be beneficial for your child, who may know this person or bump into them at some point in life. The one exception would be if you engaged in sexual sin with your spouse before marriage, and you have both agreed to share that information with your child.

To keep the conversation brief and focused, it may help to jot down some notes beforehand. Doing so can help clarify the points you will share and those you will withhold. If your child asks follow-up questions, keep your responses general and avoid getting into specifics about any one situation. If your child continues asking questions, you can respond by saying, "I love that you ask good questions, but these questions would not be helpful for me to answer or for you to hear answers to. Instead of focusing on my past sin, let's focus on God's design."

3. FOCUS

As with every conversation you have with your child about sex, the focus of this one should be on the goodness of God's design. In this conversation, you can contrast your sinful choices with God's design. For example, if you engaged in sexual relationships before marriage, you could say, "When I had sex with someone I wasn't married to, my heart, mind, and body were bonding with this person. When we broke up, it was very painful because the bond God designed to last for life was broken. I didn't realize at the time that God has placed boundaries around the gift of sex so I would not experience this kind of hurt." The purpose of framing your story in this way is to help your child see that God's commands are always for our good.

I recommend that you also focus on the goodness of God's grace. You can share with your child how grateful you are for the grace God has freely offered through Jesus's life, death, and resurrection. For example, if you struggled with a pornography addiction, you could say, "Even though I was trapped in sin for years, God has forgiven me. When he looks at me, he doesn't see someone who has been addicted to pornography. He sees the righteousness Jesus has clothed me in. How amazing is that? I didn't deserve forgiveness. No one does. But Jesus freely gave his life for me so I could be redeemed. That's incredible!" Focusing on God's grace is vital because our children are fallen too, and they will eventually struggle with different forms of sexual temptation. When they do, they need to see the truth, goodness, and beauty of the gospel. They need to be assured over and over that God is for them. He has given us his commands for our good, and he welcomes us with open arms when we repent of our sin.

. . .

Talking with our children about our past sexual sin can feel intimidating. However, when we are intentional with the timing of this conversation, the details we share, and where we place the focus, we can help our children gain a deeper understanding of both the gospel and God's good design.

22

WHAT CAN I DO TO HELP PROTECT MY CHILD FROM SEXUAL ABUSE?

Sexual abuse is a topic most of us do not even want to think about bringing up with our children. The thought of someone abusing children in this way is overwhelming, and the topic may be even more difficult to consider if you have been a victim of sexual abuse. You may fear that broaching the topic with your child will lead you to relive your painful memories. If this is where you are, my heart goes out to you, and I want to commend you for even approaching this chapter. No matter your situation right now, I encourage you to carefully think through the guardrails you can put in place to protect your child, to the best of your ability, from any form of sexual abuse. I believe there are three main ways any parent can seek to do this:

1. Equip our children to discern harmless fun from abusive and predatory behavior

2. Set boundaries to prevent opportunities for abuse

3. Train ourselves to recognize signs of abuse

Sadly, there is no foolproof plan for preventing abuse. However, implementing these three steps can help us make wise strides in protecting our children.

1. EQUIP OUR CHILDREN TO DISCERN HARMLESS FUN FROM ABUSIVE AND PREDATORY BEHAVIOR

To best protect your child, I recommend beginning these conversations around the age of four. By starting these conversations early, you are arming your child with wisdom before they reach an age where they are spending more time outside of the home or in situations where you are not present. As you could probably predict, I also recommend beginning this conversation by focusing on the positive. Start off by saying, "God has given us so many different types of good touch! Hugs, high fives, handshakes, pats on the back—these are all good types of touch. God designed these kinds of touch to help us care for one another and treat one another as his image-bearers. What are some kinds of good touch that you like?" Allow your child to describe one or more types of good touch they enjoy. You can even engage in a handshake or hug (if your child is comfortable with that) to remind them that these types of touch are good.

Next, you will want to explain that some types of touch are *not* good. An easy way to explain this is to say, "God designed so many types of good touch. However, because of sin, not all touch is good touch. Things like hitting, pushing, biting, and kicking are bad touch. These kinds of touch are hurtful and do not treat others like God's image-bearers." I recommend having your child practice this phrase: "Because of sin, not all touch is good touch." You will want them to remember this truth. You can also explain that even good touch can become bad when somebody doesn't want it. For example, if you hug someone who has asked you not to hug them, that hug has become a bad touch. To help solidify this concept, you can give your child a few examples of good touch and bad touch and have them identify which is which.

Once the above foundation has been laid, introduce the concept of sexual abuse. I recommend saying, "Remember how we have talked about God creating your body with special private parts? These special private parts of your body are the parts that your bathing suit covers. No one should ever try to see or touch these parts of your body unless your mom and I are caring for you or a doctor is examining you. And if anybody, whether an adult or another child, ever touches or tries to touch those parts of your body, that is bad touch." Ask your child if they have any questions about this. Taking time to listen and respond to their questions will allow you to address any confusion or anxiety they may have.

The next step is arming your child with a game plan for what to do if they experience sexual abuse. Tell your child that if someone ever touches these private parts of their body, your child needs to do three things: stop, run, and tell. You can say, "If someone ever touches your private parts, you should shout '*Stop!*' Then you need to *run* away and *tell* me or the nearest safe adult what happened." Practice reciting and even acting out these three steps until your child knows them by heart.

It's also important to prepare your child for how they might feel if someone ever touches them inappropriately. You can say, "If someone ever touches you in this way, you might feel scared, sad, or embarrassed. The person might tell you to keep this touch a secret, and you might want to keep it a secret because of how you are feeling. But it's so important that you do not keep it a secret and tell Mommy or Daddy right away."

Reassure your child that if they come to you and tell you what happened, you will always be proud of them for telling the truth. What's more, telling the truth will help protect them from this kind of bad touch happening again.

Even though your heart may feel heavy having these conversations with your child, doing so helps protect your child against any future abuse. As your child grows and you circle back to these conversations, it will be important to mention that most children who are sexually abused are abused by someone they know and trust (90 percent, to be exact).[1] Assure your child that even if they are not sure if someone has touched them inappropriately, it is always wisest to err on the side of caution and tell you what has happened.

2. SET BOUNDARIES TO PREVENT OPPORTUNITIES FOR ABUSE

Once we have trained our children to recognize and appropriately respond to sexual abuse, we can establish wise boundaries in our homes. One important boundary we can both teach and model is respecting the words *no* and *stop*. Children should know that when they say *no* or *stop* to any type of touch, that person should immediately stop—and the same is true for children when they touch others. (For a thorough treatment of the topic of consent, see the next chapter.)

Another important boundary is not allowing guests in bedrooms or other private spaces in the home. This means that when your child is playing with friends, they should be doing so in open communal spaces; and when you open your home to practice hospitality, bedrooms should be off-limits. Now, please do not read this as me encouraging you to view everyone outside of your family with a spirit of suspicion or as a potential threat to your child. I am *not* saying abuse is likely to occur any time children are alone with others. However, when abuse *does* occur, it is much more likely to be behind closed doors. Setting these boundaries in your home ensures that everything your child, their friends, and other guests do will happen in public spaces, making the situation safer for everyone involved.

As your child grows, some of the rules you have implemented will change. For example, in the upper elementary years, you will probably start allowing your child more alone time with friends both in your home and outside of it. As your household rules grow along with your child, you will simply want to continue the conversation about sexual abuse so your child knows the kind of things they should be aware of and what to do if they experience abuse.

Around the age of ten, it is important to begin talking with your child about inappropriate conversations. Explain that sometimes people do not begin abuse with sexual touch but rather sexual talk. I recommend having a conversation like this: "Sometimes, as children get older, adults who want to mistreat them begin with inappropriate talk instead of inappropriate touch. They might start talking about private parts or about sex before moving to inappropriate touch. If someone ever starts talking about these things with you or says things you don't understand but make you uncomfortable, get away from that person and then tell me or the nearest safe adult what happened." You will also want to help your child understand that around this age, their friends may begin talking about sex. When this happens, their friends most likely are not attempting to abuse them sexually. However, in such situations, your child would be wise to change the subject or walk away from the conversation. You can then ask your child if they have any questions about this and talk through their concerns. Preparing our children for these situations in advance can help them avoid not only sexual abuse but also grooming for such abuse.

3. TRAIN OURSELVES TO RECOGNIZE SIGNS OF ABUSE

Once we have trained and prepared our children and established healthy boundaries to the best of our ability, we also must confront the grim reality that we can never guarantee our children will be completely protected from abuse. Because of this, being observant and noting signs of potential abuse is crucial.

If a child experiences any sudden changes in behavior, mood, temperament, daily habits, or interests, this is cause to investigate. Obviously, a change in behavior and temperament doesn't automatically mean the child is being abused, but these are symptoms of abuse. If you see this type of change in your child, keep a close eye on them and start asking follow-up questions.

Unfortunately, I've seen this firsthand. A few years into my teaching career, I had a student in my third-grade class who did well academically but then started performing poorly midyear. She did not complete her assignments, was easily distracted, and spent most of her class time trying to distract other students. I consistently corrected her behavior and told her parents of my concerns, but it didn't occur to me to ask about an underlying issue. The following school year, I learned that around the time I had seen this significant change in her behavior and academic performance, she had started experiencing sexual abuse. Again, this story does not prove that every change in behavior is a symptom of sexual abuse; it simply demonstrates that we are wise to pay attention and ask questions when we see such changes in our children.

Another characteristic sign of abuse is when a child has a strong and seemingly irrational dislike for someone. As Christians, we are called to love others, and we want to encourage this in our children as well. However, if your child expresses a *strong* dislike of someone, ask them: "What makes you say that about so-and-so?" In many cases, the answer will be something insignificant—maybe another child got the prize they wanted from the prize box, or a teacher made them stay in at recess, or your child just can't explain why they don't like that person. However, sometimes, a child expressing dislike for someone can be their cry for help.[2]

As we observe our children, we should be covering them in prayer. We should pray that God would protect them, that he would grant them wisdom, and that he would give us wisdom to discern what is going on in their lives. Finally, we can rest in the fact that no matter what happens to our children, God will be faithful to his promise in Romans 8:28-29 to work all things together for our good by using all things to conform us more into the image of his Son.

• • •

We cannot guarantee our children will be completely protected from sexual abuse. However, we can proactively train our children to recognize predatory behavior. We can set wise boundaries in our homes, and we can train ourselves to recognize signs of abuse. When we take these measures, we are doing what is within our power to protect them.

23

WHAT DO I NEED TO TEACH MY CHILD ABOUT CONSENT?

Today, the word *consent* is closely linked to conversations about sexuality. In one sense, this is a good thing. As image-bearers of God, humans should not have to endure touch that is not loving or good. On the other hand, our culture often uses consent as a baseline standard for condoning violent, abusive, and even sadistic sexual acts. Because our children are growing up in a world where they will consistently hear the term *consent* used, we must help them think through this concept biblically. I believe there are two important elements to cover in this conversation: The first is the *truth* of consent as a biblical concept; we should teach our children that, as image-bearers, they shouldn't be touched in ways that are harmful or make them uncomfortable, and they shouldn't touch others in ways that are harmful or make others uncomfortable. The second is the *myth* of consent as the only moral standard for sexual activity. Our children need to understand that, in the eyes of culture, anything is permissible in the bedroom so long as there is consent—yet this is a lie. This view of consent takes sex outside of the boundaries God has placed around it and places humans in harm's way. So let's explore how we can talk with our children about both aspects of consent.

TRUTH: CONSENT IS A WAY TO HONOR FELLOW IMAGE-BEARERS

As discussed in previous chapters, we should always begin these conversations by focusing on the positive. A great place to start is with the definition of consent. *Merriam-Webster* defines consent as "compliance in or approval of what is done or proposed by another."[1] An easy way to explain this to your child is to say, "Consent is giving someone permission to do something with you or to you." Provide simple examples, such as, "When your little sister asks if she can kick the soccer ball with you, and you say yes, you have given her *consent* to play soccer with you." Or: "When Dad leaves for a work trip and asks if he can give you a hug, he is asking your *consent* to hug you."

You can then anchor this concept in the truth of humans bearing God's image. I recommend taking your child to Genesis 1:27. Discuss how God created every human in his image, and therefore, we should treat one another with kindness and respect. You can then apply this concept to physical touch. Explain that, as a general rule, no one should touch your child in a way that harms them or makes them uncomfortable, and your child should not touch others in ways that harm others or make others uncomfortable.

Of course, there are exceptions to this. For example, grabbing your child's arm to stop them from running into traffic might not be a comfortable form of touch, but it is necessary for their protection. Or, if the dentist gives your child a shot before filling a cavity, that might not be comfortable, but it is in your child's best interest. However, your child should know that, outside of such exceptions, consent is important. A simple way to explain this is to say, "As an image-bearer, your body is valuable. Before someone hugs you, they should have your consent to do so. And anytime you want to hug someone, it is important for you to have their consent." Our children should know it is okay to kindly say no when someone asks them for a hug or any other form of physical touch they do not want.

There is, however, one caveat worth adding. I have seen parents teach kids consent in a way that gives the child an excuse to only do what the child wants to do. The consent conversation teaches them to prioritize their own feelings over the feelings of others. For example, when a child visits their grandparents, their mom might say, "Okay, now it's time to give Grandma a hug." The child then responds by saying, "Nope, I don't want to give a hug right now," and walks away. This response most likely doesn't stem from proper protection of the body but from the child's sin nature. The child wants to do what the child wants to do, so they are using the concept of consent to their advantage. In those cases, I recommend giving your child some alternatives. You can say, "If you don't want to be touched right now, you don't have to give a hug. But God has called us to love others by being kind. So you can give Grandma a high five or a wave, or you can blow her a kiss." Giving our children alternatives can help them protect their bodies while training them to demonstrate kindness.

In this conversation, it is also important to cover types of touch that are never appropriate—specifically sexual touch. A simple way to explain this is to say, "If someone touches the special parts of your body that a bathing suit covers, this is bad touch. No one should ever touch these parts of your body unless Mom or Dad is helping care for you or a doctor is examining you. If anyone else touches these special parts of your body, you should immediately say 'stop,' run to the nearest safe adult, and tell them what happened."

A key follow-up to this conversation is to talk with your child about how "no" means no and "stop" means stop. Our children need to know that even if someone says no or stop playfully, we still need to honor these words. A great way to teach our children this is to model it through play. For example, if you are tickling your child and they playfully say, "Stop!" you should immediately stop and say something to the effect of, "Stop means stop, so I am not going to tickle you anymore. But if you want me to start again, just let me know." Modeling this for our children will help them understand the importance of respecting the wishes of others when they ask not to be touched.

MYTH: CONSENT IS THE STANDARD FOR SEXUAL MORALITY

The second part of this conversation involves addressing the cultural view that consent is the only and ultimate standard for sexual morality. From an early age, our children will be faced with the lie that as long as two people consent to some form of sexual activity, then that act is morally permissible.

We know from Scripture that this is a lie. God designed sex solely for the context of marriage, where sex is meant to be the loving and unifying seal of that covenant. However, the pervasive lie that consent is the only moral standard for sex is wreaking havoc on the next generation.

For example, the combination of this lie and the rising consumption of violent pornography has led to an increase in violent behaviors in the bedroom. Studies have revealed that over 20 percent of women report having been choked during sex.[2] And this number increases to 58 percent when focusing solely on college-aged women.[3] The lie of consent as the ultimate standard has led many young women to believe violent or abusive behavior is not only acceptable but normal within a sexual relationship.

Even more alarmingly, it is not just the secular world that has fallen for this lie; many within the church have fallen for it as well. Many Christian couples take this standard of consent and simply apply it to the marriage bed.[4] Anything a couple consents to is viewed as permissible—including violent behavior such as slapping, choking, or whipping. There is not space in this chapter to outline all of the biblical reasons why consent should not be the sole standard of God-honoring sex for married couples, so let me address this issue with one simple statement: If all of marriage, including the marriage bed, is a picture of Christ and the church (Ephesians 5:31-32), then any act that does not reflect Christ's self-sacrificing love for his bride has no place in the bedroom.

Now the question becomes: How do we help our children see through this lie? I think the easiest way is to give our children practical examples to consider. We can ask questions such as, "If two people agree to do something together, does that make their action right? For example, if two brothers agree to hit each other, does that make hitting okay?" You can then discuss how hitting a sibling is not treating them as an image-bearer of God, so even if the sibling being hit consents to it, the act of hitting is still wrong. Giving our children simple examples like this will help them see that consent is not the trump card for all morality.

With children twelve and older, we can tie the concept to sexuality. We can explain how many people claim that as long as two people consent to having sex or engaging in some other form of sexual activity, that action is good. Then we can ask them whether this is true. Here, it is important to remind our children that our bodies and minds are part of God's incredible design and have been designed for a purpose. As our designer, God knows what is best for us. Therefore, we look to his Word to learn the truth about how we are to flourish in our sexuality. Our world may claim that consent is the only standard, but God's Word reveals what is true.

• • •

Our children will be faced with the term *consent* from an early age. If we make time to proactively talk about this term, we can help them discern the biblical truths about this concept from the secular myths.

PART 4

WHEN LOVED ONES ARE LIVING OUTSIDE OF GOD'S DESIGN

HOW DO I TEACH MY CHILD TO LOVE OTHERS WITHOUT AFFIRMING ANOTHER PERSON'S SIN?

When I think about our current cultural landscape, I often think of a scene from one of my favorite movies, *Sense and Sensibility*. Here, the heroine, Elinor, chides her younger sister, Marianne, for openly flirting with Mr. Willoughby, a potential love interest. Marianne defends her actions but then exclaims, "Oh, Elinor, I could not bear it if you disapproved of me!" Elinor responds, "It is not you I disapprove of, Marianne, just some of your conduct."[1]

In eras past, our culture seemed to generally recognize the idea that it was possible to disapprove of someone's conduct without disapproving of the person. But today, this is no longer the case. Because our culture conflates desires with identity, disapproving of someone's behavior (which is rooted in their desires) is widely seen as equal to disapproving of the person. So how do we teach our children to graciously navigate this cultural shift while standing firm upon biblical truth?

If you have been reading these chapters chronologically, you can probably guess that I recommend starting this conversation by helping your child understand the biblical views of both sexuality and sexual sin. If you haven't yet read chapters 2 and 6, then you can start there. Have those conversations with your child first, and then come back to this chapter.

Once our children have a solid biblical understanding of both sexuality and sexual sin, our next step is teaching them how to love others who are walking in sexual sin. This begins with helping our children understand the difference between judging someone's actions and judging the person. Even for Christian adults, this can be a tricky distinction. However, a careful examination of the Bible's teachings makes the difference clear. As humans, we *are* to judge (discern) between actions that align with God's moral law and those that do not (John 7:24). Yet we are *not* to judge others by viewing ourselves as better than them (Matthew 7:1-5). Only by God's grace through Jesus can anyone be counted as righteous (Ephesians 2:8-9). So it is wrong to believe we are somehow better than others.

An easy way to help our children understand the difference between judging actions and judging the person is to use the example of a sibling doing something wrong. When a child sees his sister disobeying their parents, he can recognize (or discern) that his sister is sinning. He should not join his sister in this sin because he recognizes that what she's doing is wrong. It would also be kind for him to remind his sister of their parents' rules and encourage her to stop what she is doing. But he should not start viewing himself as better than his sister. Both he and his sister struggle with sin and are in need of God's grace.

You can then connect this concept to judging in general. As Christians, we are called to discern when actions align with God's design and when they do not. However, each of us enters this world in the same condition—as a fallen image-bearer in need of God's grace. So while we can lovingly encourage others to do what is right (and ensure we are doing right as well!), we are not to view ourselves as better than others because we are not engaging in a certain sin. This includes when we encounter others who are not following God's good design for sex, gender, marriage, or family. We can judge someone's rejection of God's good design as sin, but we are not to judge the person by viewing ourselves as morally superior.

From there, we should give our children practical action steps to take when they encounter someone who is rejecting or ignoring God's good design. In our God's Good Design Curriculum at Foundation Worldview, we teach children under the age of eight a three-step process for interacting with others who are not following God's good design: 1) recognize this is not God's good design, 2) remind yourself of the truth, and 3) be kind. Whenever little ones encounter someone living outside of God's good design—perhaps they find out that a classmate comes from a family with two dads, or they meet a little boy on the playground who is dressed as a girl, or they learn that their older cousin has moved in with her boyfriend—they can acknowledge in their minds that this is not God's good design.

The next step is reminding themselves of the truth. I recommend teaching your child simple catechizing phrases to mentally recite when they encounter sexual sin. For example, when they meet a same-sex couple, you can train them to mentally say: *God designed marriage to be one man and one woman becoming one flesh for life. God's design is so good.* When they encounter someone who is presenting themselves as the opposite gender, you can train them to say: *God designed us in his image as male or female. God's design is so good.* Such phrases, recited in their minds, will remind our children of the truth without publicly calling out another's sin. If you have a child who is a verbal processor or just loves to share information, encourage them to share the occasions when they have reminded themselves of these truths later on, when you are in private.

The third step in this process is to be kind. We can walk our children through examples of what it looks like to be kind in different situations. For example, if they learn that their classmate has two dads, they can still interact with that classmate as they would any other child. (And if they encounter their dads, they can show them the same respect they would show any adult.) Or, if they encounter a little boy at the park who is dressed as a girl, they can still invite him to play as they would any other child. The one caveat here is being kind never involves encouraging sin. For example, if our niece announces she is moving in with her boyfriend, we should not tell her we are happy for her. Doing so would be encouraging her in her sin, which is never the kind thing to do.

For children eight and older, I recommend taking them through the same three steps I outlined above, which should appropriately prepare them for many of the instances of sexual sin they will encounter. However, as your child grows, you must also prepare them for situations where they need to speak the truth in love. For example, they may be directly asked for their opinion on an issue related to the cultural conversation about gender and sexuality. They may be asked to engage in a celebration of gender and sexual identities that are not part of God's good design. Or they may need to stand up to their peers when they face pressure to watch porn, send sexual texts, or even make suggestive jokes. It can be helpful to talk to your child about different scenarios they might encounter and how they can wisely and biblically respond. (We explain this more in-depth in chapter 12, chapter 25, and chapter 32.)

Also important is teaching our children that standing for Jesus will involve suffering and persecution. In Matthew 5:11-12, Jesus said, "Blessed are you when others revile you and persecute you and utter all kinds of evil against you falsely on my account. Rejoice and be glad, for your reward is great in heaven." In 1 Peter 4:12-14, we are told,

> Beloved, do not be surprised at the fiery trial when it comes upon you to test you, as though something strange were happening to you. But rejoice insofar as you share Christ's sufferings, that you may also rejoice and be glad when his glory is revealed. If you are insulted for the name of Christ, you are blessed, because the Spirit of glory and of God rests upon you.

And Jesus assures us in John 16:33, "In the world you will have tribulation. But take heart; I have overcome the world." When your child speaks the truth in love, they may lose friends or be excluded from certain activities. But if this happens, they are in the good company of our Savior.

* * *

Loving others while still recognizing sin as sin is not easy, especially in our current culture. However, with a bit of intentionality, we can prepare our children to wisely encounter an array of situations, standing firm in both truth and love.

25

HOW SHOULD I GUIDE MY CHILD IF THEIR FRIEND COMES OUT AS GAY, LESBIAN, OR TRANSGENDER?

As our children reach the late elementary and middle school years, they will most likely have one or more friends who come out as gay, lesbian, or transgender (trans). Same-sex attraction and transgenderism are nothing new. However, because today's culture widely encourages experimenting with sexuality and gender identity, a much higher percentage of children and teens are declaring themselves to be part of the LGBTQ+ community than ever before.[1] This means our children will face many more relationships with those claiming an alternative form of sexuality or gender identity than we ever did when growing up. So how should we guide our children in thinking and living biblically when a friend comes out as gay, lesbian, or trans?

I believe the first thing we should do is help our children think through an important question: *What is the goal of friendship?* This question will help our children consider how to wisely approach their relationship with a friend who has "come out." A good way to start this conversation is by asking your child what makes someone a good friend. Discuss qualities they appreciate about their friends, such as the laughter they share, the things they enjoy doing together, how their friends stick up for them, or the times their friends have listened to and comforted them. Then you can discuss what these qualities have in common. Ultimately, the common thread is love.

The next logical question to ask is: What does it mean to love someone? This is an important question because our world promotes an altered definition of love. Today the unspoken-yet-assumed definition of love is making others *feel* good. For example, when most people talk about someone loving them, they mention how that person makes them *feel*. And, without fail, the feelings they mention are positive. The problem with this definition of love is that it doesn't account for whether such positive feelings lead to help or harm. For example, a child may feel happy when their parent says they have done good work on a school project. However, if that child hasn't truly done quality work, they'll likely receive a bad grade, and the well-meaning but untrue encouragement from their parents wasn't ultimately for their good. It would have been best for that child's parent to tell them the truth so they could correct their error before it hindered their grade.

Making others feel good is not always what is best. That is why our culture's assumed definition of love is not biblical. We see this clearly as we look at Jesus's earthly ministry. Jesus is the ultimate example of love, so when we consider what love is, we should ask ourselves: *What did Jesus do?* Was the ultimate goal of Jesus's ministry to make others feel good about themselves? No. Jesus always sought the ultimate good of others. Yet, often, this involved allowing others to feel discomfort.

A clear example of this is when the rich young ruler came to Jesus, asking Jesus what he must do to inherit eternal life. Jesus knew that this young man's possessions were of the utmost importance to him. Yet, they were keeping him from God. Mark 10:21-22 says,

> Jesus, looking at him, loved him, and said to him, "You lack one thing: go, sell all that you have and give to the poor, and you will have treasure in heaven; and come, follow me." Disheartened by the saying, he went away sorrowful, for he had great possessions.

Jesus's great *love* for this young man led him to say the one thing he knew would cause this young man great discouragement.

Similarly, when Jesus met the shunned Samaritan woman at the well, he didn't seek to make her *feel* comfortable by affirming her sin. Instead, he *loved* her by revealing her sin and her need for him. In John 4:16-18 Jesus says,

> "Go, call your husband, and come here." The woman answered him, "I have no husband." Jesus said to her, "You are right in saying, 'I have no husband'; for you have had five husbands, and the one you now have is not your husband. What you have said is true."

This interaction didn't initially lead to positive feelings. Jesus uncomfortably confronted the woman in her sin, yet that confrontation led to her salvation!

The ultimate example of Jesus's love was the cross. When Jesus was arrested, his disciples were terrified. They all fled (Mark 14:50). Even after his death, Jesus's disciples were hiding in fear (John 20:19). No part of the cross made the disciples (or Jesus!) *feel* comfortable. Yet, by going to the cross, Jesus did what was ultimately best for the disciples and for all humanity. He bore the full weight of God's wrath toward our sin so that we might be forgiven. This is true love, biblical love: giving of oneself for the ultimate good of another.

By taking our children through these biblical examples, we can help them see that our culture's definition of love is vastly different from that of the Bible. While the world views love as making others *feel* good, the Bible presents love as sacrificing ourselves for the *true* good of another.

Once our children understand that the ultimate goal of friendship is to love others, we can then discuss what it looks like to love friends who come out as gay, lesbian, or trans. (As a side note, while the conversations above can be had with any child over age seven, the following conversation is best reserved for older children once they encounter such situations or reach the age of twelve.) First, you will want to help your child think through questions they can ask their friend to better understand where their friend is coming from. Your child may first want to thank their friend for being honest with them. Then they can ask questions such as: "How long have you had these feelings? What has this experience been like for you? What made you decide to share this with others? What has been the reaction of your parents and others in your life as you have shared this information?" The goal of your child's questions is simply to learn more about the situation and let the friend know your child cares.

If your child's friend who is identifying as gay, lesbian, or trans also claims to be a Christian, loving them will involve asking follow-up questions. For example: "How does this identity fit in with your identity as a Christian?" or "Have you considered what the Bible has to say about your identity and sexuality?" The point of such questions is to learn more about their thoughts on Christianity and help them think biblically through these issues. This probably will not be a one-and-done interaction but an ongoing conversation over time. For a deeper dive into how to have these conversations, especially with teenagers, I recommend reading *Across the Kitchen Table: Talking About Trans with Your Teen* by Sam A. Andreades. Ultimately, we want to help others who claim the name of Christ see that following their fallen desires is not what is best for them. Instead, the call of the Christian is to turn from our sin and follow Jesus (Luke 9:23).

If your child's friend is not a Christian, loving them does not *primarily* involve convincing them to abandon homosexuality or transgenderism. I say this because unless they have turned from their sin and trusted in Jesus, they are still separated from God. Even if your child's friend announces they are no longer gay, lesbian, or trans, righteous living cannot save anyone. Only Jesus can (Ephesians 2:8-9). But once we come to Jesus, the Holy Spirit begins to sanctify us and empowers us to follow Jesus by obeying his commands. We should help our children see that the goal in any non-Christian friendship is to love the other person by pointing them toward their need for Jesus.

Another important conversation about boundaries is needed here. How can you ensure your child is influencing their friend without their friend having too much influence over your child? Most likely, this will require a discussion about limiting the amount of time they spend with this friend, whether in person or online. Anytime we spend a significant amount of time with someone, that person influences our thoughts, beliefs, affections, and actions. We want to make sure our children are in a place where they are able to reach out to their friends in love; but it is also important to protect them from being inappropriately influenced by lifestyles that don't align with a biblical worldview. Many times, this will involve finding another close Christian friend who can hold your child accountable. When your child has a close friend who loves God and is grounded in Scripture, that friend can help them stand firm biblically in the face of peer pressure.

• • •

As our children's friends begin embracing alternative sexual identities or lifestyles, our children must be grounded in a biblical understanding of love. This understanding will help guide their conversations and interactions with these friends.

26

HOW SHOULD I GUIDE MY CHILD IF A FAMILY MEMBER ENTERS A SAME-SEX RELATIONSHIP?

Preparing our children to face deviations from God's good design on the soccer field or in the classroom is one thing. But preparing them to face such deviations at Thanksgiving dinner or on Christmas morning is something else. Familial relationships are among the closest we have and can be the trickiest to navigate. So how can we prepare our children to think and live biblically when their uncle, cousin, grandparent, or older sibling brings their same-sex significant other home for the holidays?

If you have read and implemented the previous chapters in this book, the good news is your child is already prepared with the foundation they need for you to begin this conversation. In chapter 2, we covered how to talk with our children about God's good design for sex. In chapter 10, we looked at helping our children build a biblical understanding of marriage. And in chapter 13, we explored how to talk with our children about homosexuality. Once you have gone through these steps with your child, he or she will be ready to discuss how to interact with your family member who is now engaging in a same-sex relationship.

The first step in this discussion is to explain to your child that this family member is in a relationship with a person of the same sex. I recommend using the same language suggested in chapter 13. For example, you could say, "Can you remember what God's good design for marriage is?…That's right. Marriage is one man and one woman becoming one flesh for life. But remember how we learned that, because of sin, sometimes we desire the wrong kind of love in relationships? Sometimes people desire to be in a romantic relationship with someone who is the same sex as them. Two men or two women dating one another or marrying one another does not align with God's good design. When we go to Grandma's for Thanksgiving, we are going to see Uncle John. Right now, Uncle John is in a relationship with a man. This man will be at Grandma's with Uncle John. You might see them sitting close to one another or holding hands."

You can then ask your child if they have any questions about this. Take time to listen to your child and respond to their questions. If you are unsure of how to respond to one of their questions, you can say, "That is a great question! I am going to need some time to think about it before I answer. But we can talk more about it tomorrow."

The next step will be to discuss how your child should interact with this family member. Remind them that, as a child, it is not their job to point out others' sin. I recommend reminding them of the three steps covered in chapter 13: 1) recognize this is not God's good design, 2) remind yourself of the truth, and 3) be kind. Then you can walk through the specifics of what it looks like to be kind in this particular situation. For example, you could discuss an appropriate greeting—a smile, eye contact, "hello," and (depending on your child's comfort) a wave, handshake, high five, or hug. You could also discuss questions your child could ask this family member or things your child could share with him or her (what they are studying in school, a sport they enjoy, etc.). If your child is feeling nervous about this interaction, assure them it is okay if they stick close to you during the family gathering so you can guide their interactions.

Finally, if your child is eight or older, discuss how there may be some future interactions between you and this family member that may be difficult or uncomfortable. You can explain that, as an adult, your job is to help point this family member toward Jesus. So this may involve conversations where you, as the adult, share the truth with this family member and point them to the fact that we all are sinful and in need of redemption. If, at some point in the future, your family member becomes hostile because of your commitment to biblical truth, you can help your child understand this by reading through Scripture. Passages such as Matthew 5:10-12, John 16:33, and 1 Peter 4:12-16 reveal that following Jesus will often involve hardship and persecution. You can then explain that in this situation, your family member is upset with you or doesn't want to spend time with you because you are faithfully following Jesus. Then take your child to Romans 8:28-30 to help them see that God uses even these difficult situations for our good by conforming us more into the image of his Son. Finally, remind your child that you are still called to love this family member. So even if they are not kind to you, you will respond to them with kindness.

• • •

If we intentionally talk with our children about God's good design, as well as deviations from it, we will be prepared to explain when a family member enters a same-sex relationship. We can then focus most of our conversations around how we can love this family member and point them to Jesus.

27

HOW SHOULD I EXPLAIN TO MY CHILD WHY WE ARE NOT ATTENDING A LOVED ONE'S SAME-SEX WEDDING?

Ever since the *Obergefell v. Hodges* decision of 2015, Christians in the US have been required to make the difficult decision of whether to attend a loved one's same-sex wedding. Many devoted Christian parents, grandparents, siblings, and friends wonder if they should attend the wedding to demonstrate love and a desire to maintain the relationship. I can understand why such decisions are difficult, even heart-wrenching. However, I genuinely believe that when we investigate what it means to attend a wedding, it becomes clear that Christians cannot, in good faith, attend a same-sex wedding ceremony. For the remainder of this chapter, I will model what it would look like to help your child understand why your family is not attending a family member's same-sex wedding.

Although many conversations about sexuality should be had with children at a young age, conversations about not attending a same-sex wedding don't need to happen until a child is old enough to understand that a wedding is taking place. For some children and family situations, this might not occur until the child is twelve or older. For others, this conversation may need to occur as young as age six or seven. No matter your child's age, I recommend starting out this conversation by focusing on the positive. First, ask your child what celebrations they have enjoyed with family and friends over the years. Talk through events such as birthday parties, baby showers, graduation parties, and retirement celebrations. Discuss how, for each of these gatherings, you were celebrating a special moment or milestone in someone's life. You can then mention how weddings are also celebrations. However, unlike birthday and graduation parties, weddings are not just celebrating a special moment. During a wedding ceremony, a couple makes a covenant (a very serious promise), and everyone who attends the wedding acts as a witness to that covenant.

The concept of covenant may be new to your child, so I recommend using the Bible to help them understand it. Passages such as Genesis 15:7-20, Exodus 24:3-8, and Matthew 26:26-29 demonstrate that a covenant is a serious promise, so serious that it often involved the shedding of blood. You can then take them to Genesis 2:24 and Malachi 2:14 to help them see that marriage is also a covenant. Explain that when we attend a wedding, we are not just celebrating with the couple but bearing witness to the covenant being made. This means we are agreeing that the couple is being joined together in marriage, and we are promising to support them in that covenant.

This is where you will want to review with your child the two truths about marriage we discussed in chapter 13. Remind your child that you have already seen that marriage is one man and one woman becoming one flesh for life (Genesis 2:24). It is also a picture that represents Jesus and the church (Ephesians 5:31-32). You can then connect these truths to the upcoming family wedding by saying something to the effect of, "You remember Veronica, the woman who usually comes to Thanksgiving with Aunt Mary? Well, Aunt Mary and Veronica have decided they want to get married. According to what we have learned about marriage from the Bible, would this relationship be the kind of relationship God created for marriage?...That's right, even though Aunt Mary wants to marry Veronica, this won't be a relationship where one man and one woman become one flesh for life. And it can't be a picture of Jesus and the church. According to God's Word, even though Aunt Mary and

Veronica have decided to have a wedding ceremony, they won't really be married because God designed marriage for one man and one woman."

At this point, it would be helpful to review Leviticus 18:22, Romans 1:18-27, 1 Corinthians 6:9-11, and 1 Timothy 1:8-11 and the main talking points we covered in chapter 13. Discuss how the Bible consistently reveals that same-sex sexual relationships are sin. Talk about your love for your family member and their partner. Then discuss how the Bible has revealed that this relationship is sinful because it is not what God has designed. As with all sin, this sin is separating your loved one and their partner from God. I recommend you then take some time to pray for both individuals, asking that God convict them of their sin and their need to repent and turn to Jesus.

Next, I recommend reminding your child that a couple makes a covenant during a wedding ceremony, promising to become one flesh for life. Everyone who attends that ceremony acts as a witness to that covenant and promises to support that couple in their marriage. Then ask your child, "If our family decided to go to Aunt Mary's wedding, what would we be doing?...That's right. We would be witnesses to the covenant she is making. If we went to the wedding, we would be lying. We would be saying we agree that marriage can be between two women when God's Word reveals that marriage is one man and one woman becoming one flesh for life. We cannot lie by acting as witnesses to something God did not design. We also know that God calls same-sex relationships sin. If we went to the wedding, we would be promising to support Aunt Mary and Veronica in sin. We love God and them too much to support Aunt Mary and Veronica in sin, so we will not be going to the wedding."

It is important to follow up this conversation with a discussion about other times you will interact with your family member and their same-sex partner. I recommend saying, "Just as we already talked about, a wedding is different from any other kind of celebration because a covenant is made. We will not attend Aunt Mary and Veronica's wedding, but we will still see them many other times at holidays, birthday parties, and other gatherings. And when we see them at those events, how should we treat them?...That's right. We should love them by being kind to them. That means asking them questions about themselves and sharing things about our lives with them. We will treat them just as we treat every other family member."

We want to help our children see that while we cannot bear witness to a family member's same-sex wedding, we will still seek to be involved in that family member's life and love them by pointing them to Jesus.

• • •

If we put in the hard work up front, helping our children understand the biblical teaching on marriage and homosexuality, they will be prepared to understand why we cannot act as witnesses to the marriage ceremony of two men or two women.

28

HOW DO I PREPARE MY CHILD TO INTERACT WITH A FAMILY MEMBER OR FRIEND WHO IS TRANSITIONING?

As our culture experiences a dramatic increase in the number of youth and young adults questioning their gender identity, you may find yourself having to prepare your child to interact with someone close to you and your family who is transitioning (or has already transitioned) to another gender.[1] Such situations are never easy or comfortable. In fact, on this side of Genesis 3, most relationships are fragile and must be approached with care. However, the good news is that once we have helped our children build a biblical understanding of God's design for us as male or female image-bearers, we can easily relate these truths to real-life situations.

As we have discussed in previous chapters, helping our children love others who are rejecting or ignoring God's good design begins with helping them understand God's design and then recognizing how sin has corrupted it. For a thorough explanation of how to have such conversations regarding gender and transgenderism, please see chapter 14. The shortened version is this: Our children need to understand that God designed us as distinctly male or female, and his design is good (Genesis 1:27). However, because of sin, sometimes feelings trick us (Jeremiah 17:9; James 1:14-15). Feelings can deceive us in many ways, including the way we feel about our gender. Someone may feel they are a girl on the inside when their body reveals the truth that they are a boy (or vice versa).

Once you have laid this groundwork, you can talk with your child about your particular situation with a family member or friend who is transitioning. I recommend starting the conversation by talking positively about this loved one. Mention things that you and your child appreciate about this person, or you can bring up past fun memories you have with them. Then I recommend having a conversation that goes something like this: "In the past we have talked about the goodness of God's design for humans as male and female. We have also seen that, because of sin, feelings can trick us. We love Uncle Micah and have so many good memories with him. Right now, Uncle Micah is believing his feelings instead of the truth revealed by his body. So when we see him, things will be a little different. He will be dressed as a girl and is going by the name Michaela. Now, what is the truth about Uncle Micah? Is he a girl?…That's right. He is not a girl. His feelings are tricking him. God designed him as a wonderful male image-bearer."

At this point, you can ask your child if they have any questions. Take time to listen to what they are asking and respond. Remember, if you don't know a sound answer off the top of your head, you can simply affirm the question and explain that you will need to think about it more before answering. If your child does not have any questions, assure them that they can come to you at any point in the future if they do. Follow up by saying, "When you see Uncle Micah at our family gathering, you might feel a little bit nervous or a little bit sad. It is okay to feel these feelings. But we want to make sure we are always following the truth, not our feelings. And what is the truth about how we should treat Uncle Micah?…That's right. Uncle Micah bears God's image, and he is someone we should love."

This is a great point to remind your child of the three steps to go through when they encounter someone who is rejecting or ignoring God's good design: 1) recognize this isn't God's good design, 2) remind yourself of the truth, and 3) be kind. (For more detail on these steps, see chapter 24.) After that, discuss what being kind looks like in this situation. For example, if you are going to a birthday party for your child's uncle, who is now transitioning to present as a female, talk about how your child can smile at him and give him a hug or high five (if your child is comfortable with that). Talk about the kinds of questions your child can ask their uncle, such as, "What is your favorite birthday memory?" "How is work going?" or "Have you done anything fun lately?" You will also want to help ease any anxiety or fear your child has as they anticipate these interactions. Be sure to tell them that if they are feeling nervous or uncomfortable in this situation, it is okay if they stick close to you so they can watch how you interact with their uncle.

As you read through the above suggestions, you may have been wondering if you should simply shield your child from all such interactions and not attend events where your loved one who is transitioning is present. Every situation is different, so there is no one-size-fits-all answer as to what is best. My encouragement to you would be to spend time praying through what is best for your child, as well as what is best for your loved one. I would also encourage you to seek counsel from other godly friends and mentors in your life. It may be that, for a season, it is wisest if only you and your spouse interact with your loved one who is transitioning. It may be wisest to include your child in limited interactions. Or it may be best to continue interactions as usual while taking time to intentionally debrief with your child. No matter what you decide, you can trust that God will be true to his word and give you the wisdom you need when you need it (James 1:2-8).

. . .

As we intentionally teach our children to understand God's good design, recognize deviations from it, and love others, we are preparing them to encounter the host of situations they will encounter with family and friends, including a loved one transitioning.

29

HOW DO I EXPLAIN WHY IT'S NOT OKAY FOR A COUPLE TO LIVE TOGETHER BEFORE THEY ARE MARRIED?

Today, most couples live together before getting married. When you are in a serious relationship in our culture, it is essentially expected that you will move in together to test things out. Sadly, in many cases, cohabitating has become the norm, even within the church. This means we will all likely encounter situations where a family member or friend lives with their significant other prior to marriage. The question then becomes: How do we explain to our children that even though cohabitating with a significant other is a cultural norm, the choice does not align with God's good design?

To answer this question, I recommend taking the same three-step approach we have gone through in other chapters:

1. Build a positive biblically sound theology about God's good design for sex and marriage

2. Introduce the concept of sin and how it corrupts God's good design

3. Prepare your child to love others even when they reject or ignore God's good design

1. BUILD A POSITIVE BIBLICALLY SOUND THEOLOGY ABOUT GOD'S GOOD DESIGN FOR SEX AND MARRIAGE

First, we need to explain to our children that sex is a good gift from God, designed specifically and exclusively for marriage. As our wise Designer, God knows what is best for us and has placed these boundaries around sex for our own good. Even if we think we know the best way for ourselves, we can trust that God, our Designer, knows what is truly best for us. So when our desires go against his design, we should choose to follow his design instead of our desires. (For this discussion in full, see chapter 7.) We also need to ground our children in a biblical understanding of marriage. They should understand that marriage is one man and one woman becoming one flesh for life (Genesis 2:24), and it is a picture of Jesus and the church (Ephesians 5:31-32).

2. INTRODUCE THE CONCEPT OF SIN AND HOW IT CORRUPTS GOD'S GOOD DESIGN

Once our children have this biblical foundation, an easy way to introduce them to the concept of sin is to say, "People do not always follow God's good design. Sometimes we choose to reject or ignore it, and when we do, we are sinning. Our sin causes a separation between us and God. We see that right in the first chapters of Genesis." You can read Genesis 3 with your child and say, "What did Adam and Eve do immediately after they rebelled against God?… That's right. They realized they were naked, so they hid from God and from one another. Sin always separates us from God."

You can then connect this to sex and marriage. Explain that sometimes people reject God's good design for marriage by acting as though they are married without getting married. Take your child to Genesis 2:24, which says, "Therefore a man shall leave his father and his mother and hold fast to his wife, and they shall become one flesh." You can point out how marriage involves leaving parents and being united to one's spouse. This means a husband and wife will live together, sharing everything they own and depending on one another in a way they do not depend on anyone else. You can then explain that sometimes people choose to live with their boyfriend or girlfriend when they are not yet married. When they do this, they are acting as if they are married without entering the covenant of marriage. Most people who do this are having sex with one another. And even if they are not, they are acting as if they have entered the covenant of marriage without making that promise.

If your child is ten or older, you can discuss some of the reasons Christian couples give when they choose to cohabitate and why these reasons do not make their actions right. You can talk about how sometimes people say they are not having sex but are living together solely to save money or figure out if they enjoy living together. After you explain this, take your child to Ephesians 5:1-6. Read the passage together and discuss how sexual sin is not even to be named among Christians. You can then discuss how a couple living together gives the impression that they are having sex, even if they are not. You can follow this up by reading 1 Corinthians 6:18-20 and discussing how Christians are called to run from sexual immorality, not put themselves in situations where they will face even greater temptation. Finally, you can read Ephesians 5:31-32. Discuss how marriage is a picture of Jesus and the church and how a couple living together before marriage does not paint a picture of Jesus sacrificially loving the church.

You can also address the popular analogy used to justify cohabitating: "We wouldn't buy a car without taking it for a test drive, so why would we get married without living together first?" To help your child understand why this is a faulty analogy, ask them what a car is. Discuss how a car is an *object* designed for humans to *use* to get from one place to another. Then you can ask, "Is a boyfriend or girlfriend an *object* to be *used*?" No! A boyfriend or girlfriend is a person, a precious image-bearer of God. We test-drive cars because they are objects to use. We do not test-drive image-bearers to use them.

3. PREPARE YOUR CHILD TO LOVE OTHERS EVEN WHEN THEY REJECT OR IGNORE GOD'S GOOD DESIGN

At this point, you will want to prepare your child for the situation at hand. Most children under the age of seven will not have any idea when someone is living with another person. However, around the age of seven or eight, children become more aware of what is going on around them, and at this point, you can begin having this conversation. Explain that your family member or friend is living with their boyfriend or girlfriend. Review the reasons why this situation does not align with God's good design. Then explain that even though this person is rejecting or ignoring God's good design, your job is to love them. As I have mentioned in previous chapters, I recommend reminding your child that, as a child, it is not their job to point out others' sin. Sometimes it will be your job as an adult to lovingly point out someone's sin. However, your child's biggest job right now is to love others by being kind. You can then discuss what being kind looks like in this situation. In most situations, this simply means treating this person as you would any other person. You can also talk through specific questions your child can ask this person to show that they care about them. (This is generally a beneficial thing to do to help our children develop an awareness of and care for others regardless of the situation.)

Finally, I recommend closing this conversation by reminding your child of the goodness of the gospel. It is always helpful to remember that sin isn't just something out there in the world. Sin resides in every human heart, including our own. When we encounter sin in our hearts and lives, the proper response is to repent and turn to Jesus. And when we encounter others who are rejecting and ignoring God's good design, our biggest desire for that person should be that they repent of their sin and trust in Jesus.

• • •

Taking our children through the three steps of understanding God's good design, recognizing deviations of it, and teaching them to love others will prepare them for the host of sexual sin they will encounter in our culture, including loved ones cohabitating outside of marriage.

30

HOW DO I TEACH MY CHILD ABOUT GOD'S GRACE WITHOUT GIVING THEM LICENSE FOR SEXUAL SIN?

As we talk with our children both about God's good design for sexuality and the many deviations from that design, we must also have conversations about God's grace, especially as our children head into their adolescent years. Yes, following God's good design is what we are called to do (Deuteronomy 6:4-9; Micah 6:7-8). Yes, following that design is for our good (Psalm 1:1-2; James 1:22-25). Yes, following that design brings God glory (Isaiah 43:7; Matthew 5:16). Yet, as fallen humans, we all wrestle with the temptation to go our own way (Isaiah 53:6; James 1:14), and at times we stumble and fall (Romans 3:23; 1 John 1:8). Our children need to know that when they sin sexually, God freely offers forgiveness and redemption.

But how do we talk with our children about grace without making grace seem like a license for sexual sin? Doing this well involves two different types of conversations: 1) conversations about right belief (orthodoxy) and 2) conversations about right living (orthopraxy). As you have read through the New Testament, you may have noticed that this is the pattern taken by the authors of the epistles. Typically, the first half of an epistle explains what Christians are to believe, and then the second half describes how Christians are to live in light of these beliefs.

To ensure our children have right beliefs about sin and grace, we will want to take them directly to Scripture. Romans 3 is a great place to start. Romans 3:21-25 states,

> Now the righteousness of God has been manifested apart from the law, although the Law and the Prophets bear witness to it—the righteousness of God through faith in Jesus Christ for all who believe. For there is no distinction: for all have sinned and fall short of the glory of God, and are justified by his grace as a gift, through the redemption that is in Christ Jesus, whom God put forward as a propitiation by his blood, to be received by faith.

As you read this passage with your child, ask what truths are revealed about sin and grace. You can then discuss how this passage makes clear that all people have sinned—yet God's grace is offered freely through the finished work of Jesus. This means our good standing before God is not based on us perfectly living according to God's good design. We never could do that. We have right standing before God because of what Jesus has done for us!

A second passage that builds on these truths is Romans 5:20-21, which states,

> Now the law came in to increase the trespass, but where sin increased, grace abounded all the more, so that, as sin reigned in death, grace also might reign through righteousness leading to eternal life through Jesus Christ our Lord.

Once again, you can ask your child what truths this passage reveals about sin and grace. Then discuss how this passage reveals that God's grace reigns. This means God's grace is greater than our sin. No matter how badly we mess up, no matter how far we stray from God's good design, Jesus is ready to forgive us of our sin when we repent. God's grace has overcome! These are the right beliefs we want our children to hold about sin and grace.

From there, we want to move into conversations about right living. So what is right living regarding these truths about sin and grace? Again, let's take our kids directly to Scripture. John 14:15 is a great place to start. In this passage, Jesus is talking to his disciples and says, "If you love me, you will keep my commandments." You can read this passage with your child and ask what truths this passage reveals about how we should live in light of God's grace. Then you can discuss how this passage reveals that God's grace should lead us to love God, and this love for God should lead us to obey him. This means we should desire to follow God's good design out of our love for him. Rather than viewing God's grace as a free pass to sin, we should view God's grace as a motivation to walk in obedience.

A second helpful passage is 1 John 1:8-9, which says,

> If we say we have no sin, we deceive ourselves, and the truth is not in us. If we confess our sins, he is faithful and just to forgive us our sins and to cleanse us from all unrighteousness.

Ask your child what truths this passage reveals about how we should live in light of our sin and God's grace. Then you can discuss how this passage reveals that we will still sin even as Christians. But the proper response to our sin is confession and repentance, and God promises to forgive us. This means that even when we desire to obey God, there may still be times when we do not follow his good design. But hope is not lost. When we repent of our sin, God freely offers forgiveness.

At this point, it is important to help our children distinguish between forgiveness from God's judgment and the natural consequences that follow sinful actions. Because sexual sin carries with it serious and often life-altering consequences, we should make clear that God's grace does not erase all of the consequences of our sin. For example, if we choose to regularly engage with pornography, that will affect our sex lives, even in marriage. And healing from such an addiction may take years of rewiring our brains. If we choose to engage in sex outside of marriage, we may conceive a child. That child is a gift, but raising that child (potentially without the support of the other parent) will involve years of time, energy, and finances. Sex outside of marriage can also lead to sexually transmitted diseases and infections that have no cure.

Though God's grace is great enough to cover any sin, the consequences of sexual sin can have lasting repercussions. (For more instruction on talking with your child about the consequences of sexual sin, see chapter 9.)

After we have engaged in these conversations about right belief and right living regarding sin and grace, we can also take some practical steps at home to solidify these concepts. First, we want to ensure that we recognize all forms of sin as sin. We must be careful not to sweep offenses such as disobedience, bad attitudes, anger, or frustration under the rug. We need to recognize such things in our children (and in ourselves!) as sin. Then we must make confession, repentance, and forgiveness a way of life in our homes. Every time one of our children sins against us or a sibling, we should make sure they understand what they did was sin. Then we must walk them through the process of confessing that sin, repenting of that sin, and asking for forgiveness. This is also a process we should be modeling for our children when we sin against them. And when forgiveness is given and grace is extended, we should celebrate the restored relationship. Making confession, repentance, and forgiveness a way of life in our homes will help our children understand on a practical level that repentance and obedience are the proper responses to God's amazing grace.

· · ·

When we take our children directly to Scripture, we can help them understand right thinking and right living regarding our sin and God's grace. When we practice these truths in our home, we are helping to make right thinking and right living a way of life for our children. And we are setting them up to understand that God's grace is not to be trampled on. Grace is always extended to them and should lead them to a deeper love for our Savior and a desire to obey his commands.

PART 5

EVERYDAY QUESTIONS AND CONVERSATIONS

31

SHOULD I TEACH MY CHILD SLANG WORDS RELATED TO SEX AND BODY PARTS BEFORE THEY HEAR THEM FROM OTHERS?

f you grew up attending public school as I did, it's likely that somewhere between kindergarten and sixth grade, you were introduced to a variety of slang terms for body parts and different sexual acts. Though some of these terms have morphed over the years, you're probably not too excited about your child one day encountering them at school, from their peers, or through media. Numerous parents have approached me with this concern, asking if we should help prepare our children for such speech by directly teaching them these terms. I believe the answer to this question is yes; we should teach our children *about* these words and then use discernment as to whether we should directly *introduce* such words.

Whenever we are helping our children understand any corruption of God's good design—be it sex outside of marriage, pornography, homosexuality, slang terms, or a host of other issues—we should intentionally *prepare* our children to think and live biblically when facing that corruption without inappropriately *exposing* them to it. For example, in chapter 12, I recommend talking to children about pornography by explaining what it is, why it is not biblical, and what they can do when they encounter it. However, I obviously do *not* recommend showing children pornography to teach them what they're fleeing from. They don't need to see pornography now to recognize it later. While hearing slang terms for genitalia and sex is nowhere near as damaging as engaging with pornography, I think it is wise to take a similar approach in preparing our children to encounter both. We can do so by taking three steps: 1) focus on the good, 2) discuss why this corruption is corrupt, and 3) present a game plan for what our children can do when they encounter the corruption.

1. FOCUS ON THE GOOD

In almost every conversation we have with our children about sex, we should start off by discussing the inherent goodness of God's design. To begin this conversation, I recommend revisiting Genesis 1:27-28, which reads,

> God created man in his own image, in the image of God he created him; male and female he created them. And God blessed them. And God said to them, "Be fruitful and multiply and fill the earth and subdue it, and have dominion over the fish of the sea and over the birds of the heavens and over every living thing that moves on the earth."

Ask your child what truths this passage reveals about humans. Then you can discuss how this passage reveals the goodness of God designing us in his image as male and female and giving us the gift of sex within marriage.

2. DISCUSS WHY SLANG TERMS ARE CORRUPT

Once you have reminded yourself and your child of the inherent goodness of God's design, you can introduce the concept of slang terms for genitalia and sex. A simple way to begin the conversation is to tell your child that, because of sin, many people do not understand the goodness of God's design for our bodies or for sex. Because they do not understand that God's design *is* good, they might make fun of it and treat it like it is something goofy or even disgusting. For example, they might call a penis or vagina by another name that makes those parts of the body seem dirty or silly. Or they might take God's good gift of sex and use words to describe it that make sex seem like a joke or something bad. I think it is appropriate to explain this briefly to your child around the same age you have the first sex talk, as you will be introducing the anatomically correct terms for genitalia and explaining the word *sex*.

Once your child is over the age of seven, it is also important to explain that they may hear these terms used by people who claim to be Christians. Sadly, even some Christians don't understand the goodness of God's design. As a side note: If you have previously taught your child a nickname for their genitalia to avoid any embarrassment associated with the terms *penis* and *vagina*, you can address that you have done this, and share that you now realize this was not what is best. Giving nicknames for private parts does not treat God's design for our bodies with the honor it deserves.

A great passage of Scripture to walk through with your child is Ephesians 5:3-4. In this passage, Paul instructs Christians, "Sexual immorality and all impurity or covetousness must not even be named among you, as is proper among saints. Let there be no filthiness nor foolish talk nor crude joking, which are out of place, but instead let there be thanksgiving." You can read through these verses with your child and ask what Christians are instructed not to do. Then discuss how using slang terms for genitalia or sex would fall into the category of filthy, foolish, and crude talk. You can then explain, "You might hear these words from friends or on TV or online, but these words should not come out of your mouth."

At this point, your child may ask you what such terms are. I recommend explaining that you are not going to reveal these words because you do not want your child to have these words in their mind. However, assure them that anytime they hear a word they don't know, they can come to you. You will explain what the word means and help them determine if it is a good word or an inappropriate word.

3. PRESENT A GAME PLAN FOR ENCOUNTERING SLANG TERMS

The final step is to give your child a game plan for when they encounter slang terms. I recommend taking your child back to Ephesians 5:4, where

Scripture gives us practical advice for walking forward rightly in these circumstances: "Let there be no filthiness nor foolish talk nor crude joking, which are out of place, but *instead let there be thanksgiving*" (emphasis added). Ask your child what Christians are supposed to do instead of engaging in filthy, foolish, or crude talk. The answer to this question is that we are called to give thanks!

In the same way that we have been giving our children short catechizing phrases to privately recite whenever they encounter something that does not match God's design, we can prepare them with a short phrase of thanksgiving to say whenever they encounter sexual or anatomical slang. Explain to your child that whenever they hear a word that treats bodies or sex as if they are foolish or dirty, they can respond by quietly thanking God for the goodness of his design. For example, every time your child hears a slang term for a body part, they can mentally say, *Thank you, God, for your goodness in creating me [male or female].* Or whenever they hear a slang term for sex, they could mentally say, *Thank you, God, for designing sex for a husband and a wife.* These are also phrases that we, as adults, can use as we encounter shows, movies, social media posts, and conversations that paint sexuality in a tainted light. When we do, we can let our children know that we have practiced what we have just taught them. For example, you could say, "Last night, after you went to bed, Mommy and Daddy were watching a show, and somebody made a joke about sex because they didn't understand God's good design. So in my mind, I thought, *Thank you, God, for designing sex for a husband and a wife.*" As you put this into practice and share it with your child, you are encouraging them to continually remind themselves of the truth that God's design *is* good.

. . .

Introducing our children to corruptions of God's good design is never fun. However, by proactively preparing them to encounter slang terms for body parts and sex, we are once again grounding them in the inherent goodness of God's design and preparing them to reject the many sinful corruptions they will encounter.

32

HOW SHOULD I EXPLAIN SEXUALLY CHARGED TERMS LIKE *HOT* AND *SEXY*?

We have already explored how to handle our children encountering slang words for body parts and sex acts (see chapter 31). However, what should we do about sexually charged terms such as *hot* and *sexy* that are used so frequently in our world? Unlike slurs or curse words, these terms are not inherently sinful for us to use. But is it ever appropriate for our children to use these terms? To answer this question, we first need to think through the meanings of such words and how they are typically used.

According to *Merriam-Webster*, *hot* and *sexy* are synonyms used to describe someone or something that is "erotic" or "appealing."[1] Describing someone as erotic is not necessarily bad. Using such terms *could* be appropriate within the covenant of marriage. For example, it could be a positive thing if a wife looks at her husband and flirtatiously says, "Wow, you look really hot today," or "I'm so glad I have such a sexy husband." However, most of the time, these words are used in a way that objectifies another person, which can even be the case within marriage. More often than not, when someone describes another person as hot or sexy, they are not viewing that person as a precious image-bearer of the holy God but as an object of sexual gratification. This is why we want to help our children understand these terms and why such terms are not appropriate for them to use.

I believe it is wise to begin this conversation by focusing on the inherent value of every human. A great place to start is Genesis 1:27, which reads, "God created man in his own image, in the image of God he created him; male and female he created them." Ask your child which truth is repeated twice in this verse. Humans are made in God's image! Then you can discuss how this means that all humans have great value, dignity, and worth. Next you can take your child to Philippians 2:3-4, which says, "Do nothing from selfish ambition or conceit, but in humility count others more significant than yourselves. Let each of you look not only to his own interests, but also to the interests of others." You can then discuss how this passage reveals that we are to treat others even better than we treat ourselves. This means we should treat one another with kindness and respect.

You can then explain that, because of sin, we often do not remember that others bear God's image, and we often do not treat them with kindness or respect. Instead, we only think about what another person can do for us or what we can take from them. This is sometimes reflected in our words. Then you can introduce the terms *hot* and *sexy*. Explain what they mean and why using them does not treat others as image-bearers.

Here is a sample conversation you could have with your child: "Sometimes, rather than looking at others as God's image-bearers, people only focus on how others look and how those looks make them feel. There is nothing wrong with noticing that someone is pretty or handsome. But sometimes people *only* focus on someone else's looks and use words like *hot* or *sexy* to describe them. Those words are not good words for us to use because they are selfish and focus only on how another person's looks make us feel. So we're not going to use the words *hot* or *sexy* when describing other people. And when you hear someone use those words, try to remind yourself that the person they are talking about is an image-bearer."

We also want to make sure that our children understand that appreciating how someone looks is not a bad thing. Marveling at the beauty of God's creation is good! When we see a majestic mountain, we should marvel at it and praise God for it. When we see a brightly colored cardinal, we should marvel at it and praise God for it. When we see someone who has a pleasant physical trait, such as a warm smile, we should marvel at it and praise God for it.

You can explain this to your child and affirm something beautiful about their appearance. For example, you can say, "I love how God created your eyes to be a deep, sea green." Or: "I am so grateful God designed you with such beautiful curly black hair." We want our children to discern the difference between marveling over the goodness of God's design and treating someone as an object. I love how clear author Douglas Kaine McKelvey makes this in the liturgy "Upon Seeing a Beautiful Person" in *Every Moment Holy*:

> Lord, I praise you for divine beauty reflected in the form of this person. Now train my heart so that my response to their beauty would not be twisted downward into envy or desire, but would instead be directed upward in worship of you, their Creator—as was your intention for all such beauty before the breaking of the world.[2]

This is what we should want for ourselves and for our children—a moment-by-moment recognition that every person we encounter is an image-bearer of the holy God, fearfully and wonderfully made, for the purpose of pointing us back to the goodness of our Creator.

• • •

When we ground our children in an understanding that all humans are created in God's image, we can help them see why sexually charged terms like *hot* and *sexy* are not appropriate for them to use. And we can help them avoid the pitfalls of viewing others simply for their own gratification.

33

HOW SHOULD I ADDRESS MY YOUNG CHILD MASTURBATING?

Over the years, multiple parents have contacted me to express concern over witnessing their young (prepubescent) children masturbating. For many parents, this leads to feelings of embarrassment, shame, or confusion, but it is important to know that masturbating is not uncommon for young children. In this chapter, we will walk through specific steps to take with children of different ages if you find them masturbating. However, before we dive into the topic, I want to give a caveat: While my area of expertise is communicating complex truths to children, I am not a pediatrician or a psychologist. So if masturbation is a deeply ingrained habit in your child, I recommend consulting with your pediatrician and a Christian counselor after reading this chapter. (I will provide recommendations at the end for finding a biblically sound counselor.) Let's take a look at some practical steps to take if you discover your child masturbating at a younger age.

AGES FOUR AND UNDER

When children four years old or younger masturbate, it is usually a form of self-soothing. Children this young are in a stage of discovering their body parts and what those parts do. Frequently, they touch different parts of their body to comfort themselves before falling asleep or when they are feeling sad;

many children suck their thumbs, others stick their fingers up their noses, and some play with their genitalia. At this stage, the best way to react to masturbation is to treat it as you would any other socially inappropriate behavior. For example, if you found your three-year-old picking his nose, you would say, "It's not appropriate to have your finger in your nose. So we're not going to do that." Then you would gently pull his finger out of his nose. Similarly, if your three-year-old has his hand inside his pants, you should gently remove it and say, "It's not appropriate to have your hand in your pants. So we're not going to do that."

Just as children with the habit of thumb-sucking or nose-picking usually need help breaking the habit, your young child will probably need some help breaking the habit of masturbating. It can be helpful to give your child something else to do with their hands when they are trying to fall asleep or are feeling sad. For example, you could give them a soft stuffed animal, a fluffy blanket, or a stress ball to hold. These kinds of objects are tactile and (as long as they are not choking hazards) can be helpful self-soothing replacements.

It is also important to note that at this stage of child development, children need lots and lots of appropriate physical affection. Such physical affection from Mom and Dad can go a long way in helping break any unhealthy self-soothing habit. So even if you are not the most touchy-feely person, try to give your child plenty of hugs, kisses, and snuggles.

AGES FIVE THROUGH EIGHT

If your child is over the age of four, learning that they are masturbating may come as more of a shock. However, it is very important to keep a calm and positive demeanor when you address this issue with them. If you respond with shock or disgust, your child may feel embarrassment or shame and then continue this pattern in secret. Responding calmly may require you to take a deep breath or even walk out of the room momentarily to gain your composure. However, it is important to address the behavior right then by saying something such as, "I noticed that you just had your hands inside your pants touching your penis [or vagina]. Remember how we talked about your penis [or vagina] being a very special part of your body? This is the part of your body God designed for the good gift of sex in marriage. But right now, the only time you should touch this part of your body is when you are using the bathroom or cleaning yourself."

After discussing it once, move on without making this conversation a big deal that will cause your child to feel embarrassed or ashamed. However, if this behavior becomes a pattern, ask your child questions to understand the root issue that is leading them to masturbate. You can ask, "How are you feeling inside when you do this?" Give them some options to help them respond: Are they feeling sad? Lonely? Scared? Bored? Your child might tell you how they feel, or they might not even know what they feel. In this case, you can say, "It's okay if you don't know what you are feeling. But the next time you feel like playing with your penis [or vagina], I want you to think, *Hmm, what am I feeling inside that's making me want to touch this part of my body?*"

Once your child can identify the root feeling that is leading to masturbation, you can give them an alternative technique to address that underlying issue in a healthy way. If they're touching themselves to respond to sadness, talk through alternative responses such as singing a song, reading a book, or hugging a stuffed animal. If they feel lonely, they could find a sibling to play with or a picture to color and give to a friend or neighbor. If they are scared, they could recite a Bible verse or hug a family member. If they are bored, they could do another activity they enjoy, such as reading, coloring, or playing a game.

AGES NINE TO TWELVE

If your child is masturbating between the ages of nine and twelve, you will need wisdom to discern if they are doing this in response to an emotion such as sadness, fear, or loneliness or whether this is coming from a sexual desire. If you think your child's masturbation stems from an emotional response, I recommend going through the same steps recommended for children ages five through eight, helping them to first identify their emotions and then think through healthy alternative responses.

If you believe their masturbation stems from sexual desire, I recommend you read chapter 11 and begin talking with your child about the biblical purpose of sex and why masturbation isn't part of God's good design. Talk to your child about what it means to guard their thoughts, as most sin begins in the mind. I recommend you work with them on memorizing passages of Scripture that will help them focus on what is true and good. A great place to begin is Colossians 3:12-17. You can also talk through readily available activities they enjoy and can go to when they are tempted to masturbate. The goal here is to give them something to occupy their time and attention so they're not focusing on the temptation to masturbate.

One last caveat: While it is not uncommon for prepubescent children to masturbate or feel curious about their genitalia, if this behavior in your child has emerged suddenly and occurs frequently, or if you think that what they are doing falls outside the bounds of normal development, I strongly encourage you to seek professional help. Talk to your child's pediatrician in addition to seeking help from a Christian counselor. BiblicalCounseling Center.org is a great resource if you're looking for a biblical counselor. The website will direct you to set up a virtual appointment with a certified biblical counselor. Focus on the Family also has a counseling hotline. If you call them at 1-800-A-FAMILY, they can connect you with a counselor who can provide you with resources and guidance.

• • •

Discovering children masturbating can be disconcerting. However, you can take wise steps to help discern the root cause and determine if further guidance from a pediatrician and counselor is necessary.

34

IS A BOY WEARING A DRESS THE SAME AS A GIRL WEARING PANTS?

A parent wrote into the *Foundation Worldview Podcast* asking, "How should we guide our children when seeing men or boys wearing dresses, pearls, makeup, nail polish, et cetera?" The parent went on to say,

> Seeing this makes me uncomfortable and it's becoming more prevalent, but I don't really know which Bible verses would be relevant as to why it's wrong. I also keep thinking back to what people must have been saying when women wanted to wear pants, when dresses were more acceptable. I don't have a problem with women wearing pants. How should I deal with this?

In today's culture, not only is this an important question for parents to think through, but the way it is worded addresses something we often run into as Christians. Sometimes things *feel* wrong or make us uncomfortable, but we haven't spent enough time thinking through them to know if they are *actually* unbiblical. In these situations, we should always spend time in God's Word to see whether our concern is just something that makes us uncomfortable or something that truly contradicts Scripture. Too often we make the mistake of coming to our own conclusions and then turning to the Bible and finding random verses to support our opinions. Instead, we should approach Scripture with humility and a willingness to submit ourselves under its authority, regardless of whether it aligns with our feelings. This is something we want to train our kids to do as well.

The good news is, when it comes to this question—*how should our gender inform our dress?*—the Bible offers us clear guidance. Deuteronomy 22:5 reads, "A woman shall not wear a man's garment, nor shall a man put on a woman's cloak, for whoever does these things is an abomination to the LORD your God." In this verse, the Hebrew word translated as *abomination* signifies something that is wicked. You may wonder why cross-dressing would be considered wicked. To understand this, we must look at the verse in its broader context. Deuteronomy literally means "second law." It is a retelling of the whole law that God gave to the nation of Israel at Mount Sinai. This law began in Exodus 20 with the Ten Commandments, and most other commands in the Mosaic Law are anchored in these ten. Two of these commands directly address the issue in question—the ninth commandment, which forbids lying, and the tenth commandment, which forbids coveting (Exodus 20:16-18). In light of these two commandments, we can more fully understand why God calls dressing as the opposite sex an abomination. First, cross-dressing is a form of deception; the intention behind it is to be perceived by others as a member of the opposite sex. Second, cross-dressing is a form of coveting. When a man wears women's clothes, or vice versa, this represents an inner desire to reject one's own body and instead have the body God had assigned to the opposite sex. Because cross-dressing breaks these two commandments, it is something God considers wicked.

The question now becomes, why do we consider men wearing dresses cross-dressing but not women wearing pants? Are women in violation of Scripture if they wear pants? That is an important question to consider. To answer this, we should look at the two commandments that cross-dressing breaks—lying and coveting—and ask ourselves if women are violating either commandment by wearing pants. First, when a woman wears pants, is she attempting to convince others that she is male? Typically, the answer is no. There may be some women attempting to pose as men, but to do so, they need to do much more than simply throw on a pair of jeans. Even when women first began wearing pants in the early twentieth century, their motivation was not to deceive. Next, we need to ask, when a woman wears pants, is she expressing an inward coveting of the male body? It could be argued that the women who initially wore pants in the early twentieth century were coveting both the body and roles of men. However, nowadays, this is not typically the case. Pants have become a culturally appropriate expression of femininity. This is evidenced by the fact that when I shop for jeans, I head to the women's department and purchase jeans specifically designed for the female body. Should dresses and skirts one day become a culturally appropriate expression of masculinity, men wearing them would not be in violation of these biblical principles.

We see this even as we think of current cultures in which dresses or skirts express masculinity. For example, in Scotland, kilts are a masculine form of dress. Similarly, in Bhutan, the gho, a long dress-like robe, is traditional male garb. Even in today's Western culture, there are ways that men might wear dress-like garments that are not attempts to deceive or expressions of coveting. For example, a young man graduating from high school will wear a graduation gown. A man having a procedure done at the hospital will wear a hospital gown. A man relaxing at home after a long day may sport a bathrobe. None of these are gender-bending deceptions that will lead others to mistake them for women or expressions of an inward coveting of the female form. Should other types of dresses or skirts one day become distinct forms of expressing masculinity, such garments would not automatically express deception or envy.

Now the question becomes: How do we prepare our children to think biblically when they encounter men and boys who are dressing as females? In this situation, we should follow the same formula I have suggested throughout the book—introduce God's good design, then explain how sin has corrupted it. The first step in this process is to once again affirm the goodness of God's design for males and females. You can revisit Genesis 1:27 with your child and discuss how this verse reveals the truth that God designed all humans in his image as male or female. Then you can discuss how these are not choices we get to make. Like it or not, God designed all humans in his image, and he decided whether we would be male or female. The next step would be to take your child to the passages referenced above, Deuteronomy 22:5 and Exodus 20:16-18. Read through these passages with your child and discuss the truths revealed—how we are not to dress as the opposite sex because doing so is a form of lying and coveting.

Once the above foundation has been laid, you will want to prepare your child for times when he or she encounters someone who is cross-dressing. I recommend implementing the same strategy highlighted in chapter 24: 1) recognize this is not God's good design, 2) remind yourself of the truth, and 3) be kind. These steps will help further ground your child in the truth, while also reminding them that our calling as Christians is to love others.

But what should you do if your son suddenly expresses interest in wearing clothing or other items traditionally associated with female dress? I think you should help him think through why he desires such things. For example, if your ten-year-old son comes home from school wanting to paint his fingernails, ask why he wants to do this. Is he seeking to deceive others into believing he is female or associating himself with femininity? If the answer is yes, then the nail polish is a definite no. If the answer is no, you should then ask if he is expressing an inner desire to be female or feminine. Again, if the answer is yes, the nail polish is a definite no. But if the answer to this question is a no, you should try to figure out why he wants to do this. Maybe all his friends are painting their fingernails. Or maybe he just thinks it would be fun to have brightly colored fingernails. At this point, you will need to implement wisdom. You may think it is okay for your son to engage in artistic expression by painting his nails. Or you may decide this is something you are not comfortable with. If this is the case, you should explain to him why you are not comfortable with this and why he will not be allowed to paint his fingernails while living in your home. Then follow up by explaining that what he desires to do is not inherently sinful. So when he grows up and is out on his own, he can choose to paint his fingernails. Making these kinds of distinctions will help your child think biblically, understanding when something is clearly sin and when it is a matter of conscience.

. . .

When we understand that cross-dressing breaks the commandments against lying and coveting, we can help our children understand why cross-dressing goes against God's good design. And we can help guide our children in the clothing in which they choose to present themselves.

35

IS IT OKAY FOR MY CHILD TO PRETEND TO BE THE OPPOSITE SEX WHEN PLAYING DRESS-UP?

Three decades ago, nobody gave it a second thought if a little girl put on her dad's shoes and tie to play dress up. Such an action was considered nothing short of adorable. However, with so many (justified) concerns around the topic of gender today, many parents wonder whether it is okay for their children to pretend to be the opposite sex when playing dress-up. I think we can answer this question with clarity when we first think through the answer to another question: What is the *motivation* behind dressing up as the opposite sex? For the remainder of this chapter we will explore different possible motivations for children dressing up as the opposite sex and how we can wisely respond.

DRESSING UP TO FILL IN A GAP

One motivation your child might have for dressing up as the opposite sex is that they are playing a game or imagining a situation where someone of the opposite sex is needed but not available, so they are filling in the gap. For example, when my sister was young, another little girl from our church frequently came over to play with her on Sunday afternoons. During these playdates, they liked to dress up and have a pretend wedding. Because my sister was taller than her friend, she was always the groom. So they would both dress up in their respective costumes and pretend to get married. All of this was harmless fun. My sister wasn't expressing a desire to be a boy or marry a girl. She just liked weddings and wanted to pretend to have one. You might see this with your children as well. For example, if you have all daughters and they're playing house together, one of them might pretend to be the dad because they don't have a brother who can play that role. If this is your child's motivation, this shouldn't be a cause for alarm.

DRESSING UP TO EMULATE AN OLDER SIBLING

Another motivation for dressing up as the opposite sex is a desire in younger siblings to emulate their older siblings of the opposite sex. For example, several of my close friends with three children have two girls and one boy or vice versa. In these families, I have watched the youngest siblings dress up in opposite-sex costumes just to fit in with their older siblings. These friends' daughters have not truly sought to be male pirates, nor have their sons sought to be princesses. They chose to wear such costumes simply to join in a game of pretend with their older siblings. Because these friends have wanted to encourage their children to embrace and celebrate their God-given gender, they have wisely purchased costumes that would allow their youngest child to join in their older siblings' fun while still dressing as a character of their sex. For example, one friend bought her son a knight costume so that he could join his sisters while they played princess, and another friend bought her daughter a female pirate costume so she could join her brothers on pretend treasure hunts.

DRESSING UP FOR A LAUGH

Another motivation for dressing up as the opposite sex could be that children think it's funny. A girl might put on her dad's suit jacket and talk in a really low voice, or a boy might put on a skirt and high heels and act like a girl just to get a few laughs. This desire for humor isn't a cause for concern, but I think it is a reason to have an intentional conversation about the goodness of God's design. For example, if your son dresses up as a girl for laughs, you can gently tell him, "I love that you have a great sense of humor and want to laugh. But remember, God designed you as a boy, and God's design for you is so good. God's design for girls is also good. We do not want to make fun of what God designed to be good. So I don't want you to play like that anymore. Let's find other ways to use your great sense of humor."

DRESSING UP WITHOUT A CLEAR MOTIVATION

One motivation that might be a cause for concern—though not panic—is if your child consistently gravitates towards opposite-sex costumes for no apparent reason. This, again, is a situation where you will want to have an intentional conversation. For example, if your daughter is consistently dressing up as a boy when she is not needed to play a male role or when female costumes are available, you could say, "I've noticed that when you are playing dress-up, you always want to be the boy character. Do you think there is a reason for why you like to do this?" Then provide her with an opportunity to share why she does this. You can then follow up by saying, "God designed you as a girl, and God's design for you is good. So when you're playing dress up, even though you are just pretending, you should still pretend things that follow God's good design for you. When you dress up, I want you to dress up as characters who are girls."

It is important to recognize that a child can dress up as something that isn't traditionally associated with their gender but is still available to their gender. For example, most firefighters are men, and most firefighter costumes are marketed to boys. However, if your daughter wants to dress up as a firefighter, that's okay because there are female firefighters, and a firefighter isn't an inherently gendered role (unlike a princess or a king). Similarly, most elementary school teachers are women, but men can also teach. So if your son enjoys playing school and pretending to be a teacher, that is fine, as long as he is not specifically pretending to be a female teacher.

DRESSING UP IN ADMIRATION OF A CHARACTER

One final situation that might be a bit trickier is when a child becomes fixated on dressing up as a well-known character of the opposite sex. For example, a girl might enjoy dressing up as Darth Vader, or a boy might enjoy dressing up as Elsa. There is nothing inherently wrong with a child being drawn to such fictitious characters. However, it is still wise to have conversations similar to the ones modeled above, reminding your child of the goodness of God's design for them and the importance of celebrating that design even when playing. Then you can point your child to another character from that movie or series who *is* their gender (such as Princess Leia or Kristoff).

As you have these redirecting conversations with your child, it is important to remember that we cannot expect our children to learn everything in one conversation. Think about when you are training your children in other things, such as using the toilet, tying their shoes, setting the table, or taking out the trash—this training requires consistent practice. Even after having an intentional conversation with your child, there is a chance that they may still dress up as the opposite sex again. If they do, that is an opportunity to once again model the love of Christ and gently talk to them again about why it is good to honor God's design for them while playing dress-up.

• • •

If we find our children dressing up as characters of the opposite sex, we are wise to first determine the motivation behind such actions. When we have a clear understanding of their motivation, we can determine when such actions are appropriate and when they require redirection.

36

HOW CAN I ENCOURAGE MY CHILD WHO DOESN'T FIT IN WITH TRADITIONAL GENDER NORMS?

If your child doesn't fit within traditional gender norms, you may worry that they'll one day get swept up in our culture's gender confusion and wonder if you should begin encouraging them toward behaviors that align with traditional norms. While this situation can feel daunting, there is some good news—God's Word offers direction, showing us that true masculinity and femininity are more nuanced and more beautiful than any cultural stereotype. If you find yourself in this situation, wondering how to guide a son or daughter who doesn't fit into the traditional mold, I believe there are four important steps you can take: 1) affirm your child's design as distinctly male or female, 2) ground your child in the biblical teachings on maleness and femaleness, 3) encourage your child's giftings as distinctly male or female, and 4) offer gentle redirection where needed. Let's discuss each step and how to apply it with your child.

1. AFFIRM YOUR CHILD'S DESIGN AS DISTINCTLY MALE OR FEMALE

If your child is under the age of seven, chances are they have not yet noticed that their giftings, personality, and/or interests do not align with those of their same-sex peers. However, even at this young age, you can begin affirming the goodness of your child's design as distinctly male or female. This can be done in simple ways every day. For example, whenever your child does something well, you can phrase your encouragement by saying, "You did such a good job at _____. I am so grateful that God made you a girl (boy) who is good at _____." Setting this framework for the goodness of their design as distinctly male or female will help your child in future years when they may feel left out or like they do not fit in.

As your child grows and becomes more socially aware, it will become important for you to continue this encouragement. If your child expresses frustration over not fitting in or feeling different, you can affirm the goodness of God's design for them by taking them directly to Scripture. Psalm 139:13-16 reads:

> For you formed my inward parts;
> you knitted me together in my mother's womb.
> I praise you, for I am fearfully and wonderfully made.
> Wonderful are your works;
> my soul knows it very well.
> My frame was not hidden from you,
> when I was being made in secret,
> intricately woven in the depths of the earth.
> Your eyes saw my unformed substance;
> in your book were written, every one of them,
> the days that were formed for me,
> when as yet there was none of them.

You can read this passage with your child and discuss the many truths revealed, mainly that God purposely designed them well and ordained all their days beforehand. Then discuss how both their design as male or female and their personality and giftings are not accidental. God has specific and good plans for them.

2. GROUND YOUR CHILD IN THE BIBLICAL TEACHINGS ON MALENESS AND FEMALENESS

Christians can easily become confused about what it means to be distinctly male or female because the Bible does not contain long lists of qualities that are distinctly male or distinctly female. In fact, most of the commands in Scripture are for both men and women, meaning godly men and godly women will share many of the same characteristics. However, the Bible does make clear that there are differences between males and females. As followers of Jesus, we should stick closely to the text of Scripture, holding to the truths it reveals about maleness and femaleness while not making up rules or roles that go beyond the teachings of Scripture. There is not space in this chapter to explore an exhaustive teaching on maleness and femaleness as presented in Scripture. However, there are a few important truths to cover with our children.

The first truth to cover is that God designed men with the capability of becoming husbands and fathers and women with the capability of becoming wives and mothers (Matthew 19:4-6). This does not mean that all children will grow up, get married, and have children. But it does mean that God created them with that potential. A simple way to present this to our children is to explain that when they become adults, they may get married and have children. If this happens, they will then take on a new role as husband or wife and father or mother. You can then take your child to Ephesians 5:22–6:4 to explore what it means to be a husband, wife, father, or mother who honors God.

The next truths to cover are some basic commands that God has given specifically to males and specifically to females. The following is not an exhaustive list of male or female-specific biblical commands, but I believe it is a good place to start. For our boys, I recommend taking them to Titus 2:2, which reads, "Older men are to be sober-minded, dignified, self-controlled, sound in faith, in love, and in steadfastness." After reading this passage together, we can then discuss what truths this passage reveals about being a godly man. Our sons should strive for these qualities as they seek to be men who honor God. Other helpful passages to take them to are 1 Peter 3:7, 1 Timothy 2:8, 1 Timothy 3:1-5, and Titus 1:6-9. The final two recommended passages specifically address qualifications for overseers/elders, but the characteristics listed are qualities all men should strive for.

Titus 2:3-5 is a great passage to take our daughters to. It reads,

> Older women likewise are to be reverent in behavior, not slanderers or slaves to much wine. They are to teach what is good, and so train the young women to love their husbands and children, to be self-controlled, pure, working at home, kind, and submissive to their own husbands, that the word of God may not be reviled.

After reading this passage together, we can discuss what truths this passage reveals about being a godly woman. Our daughters should strive for these qualities as they seek to be women who honor God. Other helpful passages to walk through with daughters are 1 Timothy 2:9-10 and 1 Peter 3:1-6.[1]

3. ENCOURAGE YOUR CHILD'S GIFTINGS AS DISTINCTLY MALE OR FEMALE

Once your child is grounded in a biblical understanding of what it means to be distinctly male or female, you can then encourage them to continue developing their natural giftings as distinctly male or female. For example, if you have a son who is gentle and artistic, encourage him in the way you see his gentleness and creativity reflect God's call for him to be a godly man. As he interacts with others in gentleness, affirm that you see him following the Titus 2 call for men to be self-controlled and steadfast in love. As he creates art that reflects the goodness of God, affirm that you see him follow the Titus 2 command for men to be dignified and sound in faith. If you have a confident and athletic daughter, encourage her in the way you see these qualities reflect God's call for her to be a godly woman. As she confidently interacts with others, affirm that you see her following the Titus 2 command for women to not slander others and to be kind. As she continues to grow in her athletic ability, affirm that you see her following the Titus 2 command for women to be reverent and self-controlled.

One of the most beautiful things about biblical masculinity and femininity is that it is not one-dimensional. God has given specific commands to males and females and then gifted us with a host of different personality traits and strengths that we are to use for his honor and glory. We should strive to help our children see that they have the amazing privilege of using their personality and strengths according to God's design for them as distinctly male or female.

4. OFFER GENTLE REDIRECTION WHERE NEEDED

Even after going through the three previous steps, you may still observe some behaviors in your child that need redirecting. For example, you may find that your daughter solely has male friends. While it can be wonderful to have friends of the opposite sex, it would be wise for her to develop at least one friendship with another girl. Or you may find that your son's gentle nature causes him to always take a back seat and let others lead. While having an agreeable and easygoing personality is often a blessing to others, always going with the flow may one day lead your son to cave into peer pressure and compromise on what Scripture has called him to. So it would be wise for him to work toward growing in confidence to lead.

If you encounter situations like these where you need to gently offer redirection, I recommend you first pray for wisdom in how to do so and then help your child make such changes. For example, if your daughter solely has male friends, pray first for wisdom about which friendships to encourage. Then be intentional at providing her with opportunities to get to know those other girls better, whether by having other families over to your house for dinner or setting up play dates. Or, if your son always takes a back seat and doesn't lead, pray for wisdom in how to guide him in this area. Then be intentional about placing him in situations where he can grow in leading. For example, if your son has younger siblings, assign him simple leadership tasks with them, such as helping them get ready in the morning, working with them on a memory verse, or teaching them a new skill.

* * *

If your child doesn't fit into the stereotypical mold of traditional gender norms, you need not fear. As you affirm their maleness or femaleness, ground them in Scripture, encourage their giftings, and offer gentle redirection, you will help them see the goodness of God's design for them.

37

HOW DO I ENCOURAGE SEXUAL MODESTY IN MY CHILD WITHOUT INTRODUCING SHAME?

The topic of modesty can be a tricky one to navigate. What has now been dubbed the "purity culture" of the late 1990s and early 2000s placed a big emphasis on the idea of modesty in dress, particularly for girls. Many have criticized the movement for teaching this message in ways that made females feel shame over their bodies, and you'll hear some today claim that any and all teachings on modesty are harmful. While my mom did a great job of pointing me to biblically sound teachings on modesty, there were several moments during my growing-up years when other well-meaning Christians made comments about my clothes that led me to feel like my developing body was inherently shameful and should be hidden. Because of this, I can empathize with those who feel that purity culture's teachings on modesty were harmful. If you received unbiblical and harmful teachings on modesty during your growing-up years, I am so sorry. I applaud you for even taking the time to engage with this chapter. As we invest time exploring the concept of modesty, I want to encourage us not to throw the idea of modesty out the window but, instead, to explore what the Bible teaches on the topic and how we can impart that to our children.

If you searched for the word *modesty* or *modest* in an English translation of the Bible, you would arrive at a very short list of verses—two, to be exact (1 Corinthians 12:23; 1 Timothy 2:9). However, this does not mean modesty is unimportant to God. Looking at the definition of modesty reveals that while the word is scarcely referenced, the *concept* is woven throughout Scripture.

According to *Merriam-Webster*, modesty is "propriety in dress, speech, or conduct,"[1] and you have probably noticed that the Bible has a lot to say about what we do in those areas! In fact, most books of the Bible provide instructions on how we are to live in ways that honor God. And one of my favorite things about Scripture is that it doesn't just list what we should and should not do, but it reveals *why* such commands are right and good. When thinking through biblical propriety in speech, conduct, and dress, all commands given in these areas are anchored in the fact that God alone is worthy of worship (Exodus 20:3; Isaiah 42:8; 1 Timothy 1:17; Revelation 4:9-11). As his image-bearers, it is our responsibility and privilege to live in a way that brings him glory (Genesis 1:26-27; Psalm 115:1; Luke 4:8). This means all we think, say, and do should point others to him. This is true modesty.

Though you may not have thought about it this way before, attempting to draw others' attention toward ourselves—being immodest—is, in effect, equivalent to seeking to steal glory from God. To use an example from my own life, I often struggle with immodesty in my storytelling. God has designed me as a natural-born storyteller, and I love using this gift to draw people in as I relay different events from my life. However, when telling such stories, I am frequently tempted to make myself the focus of these stories. Whenever I do this, I am taking attention away from the goodness of God and placing it on myself. Instead, I should seek to tell each story truthfully for the purpose of pointing others to God's goodness and faithfulness in my life. This would be true modesty.

As we think about helping our children develop a biblical understanding of modesty, I believe we should begin with this concept of God's worthiness and our responsibility to point others to him. You can read through the passages of Scripture referenced above and ask your child what these passages reveal about God and our relationship to him. You can then discuss how our goal in all that we think, say, and do should be to give glory to God—to point ourselves and others toward his goodness. Once this foundation is laid, you can begin discussing what this should look like in different areas of life. I recommend having conversations about how to apply the concept of modesty in the three areas highlighted in the definition: speech, conduct, and dress.

1. MODESTY IN SPEECH

As with any conversation we have with our children that relates to sexuality, we want to begin this one by focusing on the goodness of God's design. I recommend you take your child to passages of Scripture such as Proverbs 15:1-4, Proverbs 16:24, and Ephesians 4:29 that talk about the goodness of God's design for our speech. You can then link this back to the concept of modesty. Ask your child what it would look like to steal glory from God through our speech. Then discuss how any speech that solely focuses on us or seeks to inappropriately gain the attention of others is immodest. You can give specific examples, such as bragging about how well you did in a soccer game versus joyfully sharing that information while mentioning how grateful you are that God designed our bodies to be able to play soccer. Or talking really loudly so that everyone in the room focuses on you versus asking others questions to get to know them better and then sharing information about yourself so that they get to know you.

If your child is ten or older, you can connect modesty in speech to sexuality. I believe there are two important concepts to focus on in such conversations. First, we should help our children understand that as they begin to develop an interest in the opposite sex, they may be tempted to speak in ways that draw attention to themselves. For example, when someone they are interested in comes around, they may be tempted to start talking more loudly to gain the attention of that person. Or they may begin to start talking about themselves and their accomplishments. Instead of doing this, they should focus on honoring God through getting to know the other person as a friend and seeking to point that person toward the goodness of God. They can do this by asking the other person questions and then humbly sharing their own thoughts and opinions.

The second area I believe is important to focus on is how they speak *about* others—and even about themselves. As our children grow, they will likely encounter situations where their peers are making objectifying and often sexually charged comments about either the desirability and experience of others or of themselves. We might call this locker room talk, bragging, or gossip, but the effect is the same. We will want to help our children see that this type of unwholesome talk or any other form of speech that treats others as objects rather than image-bearers is not honoring God. It steals glory from him by focusing on how others make us feel rather than on the goodness of God's design for that person.

2. MODESTY IN CONDUCT

After we have addressed modesty in speech, we will want to talk with our children about modesty in their conduct. Once again, I recommend beginning the conversation with the goodness of God's design. You can take your child to passages of Scripture—such as Philippians 2:1-5 and Colossians 3:12-17—that talk about God's good design for our conduct. You can then link this back to the concept of modesty. Ask your child what it would look like to steal glory from God in our conduct. You can then discuss how any conduct that does not accurately reflect God and point others toward him would be immodest. You can give examples such as acting pridefully after winning a game, treating others disrespectfully, or talking to others with unkind words.

If your child is ten or older, you can connect modesty in conduct to sexuality. I recommend you begin the conversation by asking them to list some of the corruptions of God's good design for sexuality that you have discussed in the past, such as sex outside of marriage, pornography, and homosexuality. You can then talk about how engaging in any of these corruptions is immodesty in conduct—it is stealing glory from God by not representing him or his good design correctly to others. As your child enters their adolescent years, I recommend broadening the conversation by discussing how any action that seeks to draw sexual attention from others (outside of marriage, of course) is immodest. You can then talk through what it will look like for your child to act modestly in their conduct with the opposite sex. Talk through the different situations they will likely face and how they can point others to God's goodness in each situation.

3. MODESTY IN DRESS

Modesty in dress is, without a doubt, the trickiest part of this discussion. I recommend beginning this conversation by discussing the inherent goodness of our bodies. You can take your child to different Scripture passages—such as Genesis 1:26-31, Psalm 139:13-16, and 1 Corinthians 6:19-20—and discuss how God designed our bodies well. Then discuss how the inherent goodness of our bodies connects to the concept of modesty. I recommend saying something like, "God made our bodies in such an amazing way. And he designed our bodies to bring him glory. One of the ways we can bring him glory is through how we dress. This means we are going to choose clothes that won't make people stare at us and focus only on how we look. For example, we aren't going to wear footy pajamas to the swimming pool or a bathing suit to the grocery store. Wearing those clothes in those settings would seem very strange and would draw a lot of attention to ourselves. Instead, we want to dress in clothes that help point the attention back to God by not having people focus on how we look."

If your child is ten or older, you can begin having conversations that connect the concept of modesty with sexuality. I recommend that such conversations again begin with the inherent goodness of God's design for their body. Then you can discuss how our world doesn't understand God's good design for sexuality, and because of that, it encourages us to focus on how much we enjoy looking at others' bodies, as well as how much attention we can get from others with our bodies. But neither of these is where we should focus. You can then explain that when we look at others' clothing, we should not be focusing on how much we enjoy or do not enjoy their bodies. And when we choose our clothing, our main goal shouldn't be to attract the attention of others to our bodies. Discuss how your child's body is precious and valuable. Therefore, you want to help him or her dress in a way that honors their body and helps them point others toward God's goodness. You can explain that even when we seek to be intentional in our clothing choices, others may not agree that what we choose to wear is modest. (I am pretty conservative in my attire, but I once attended a wedding where I received dirty looks from others who held different modesty standards.) However, our goal is not to meet the approval of every other person but to seek to honor God through what we wear. If our conscience is clean before God, we need not fear if someone has a negative opinion of what we wear.

It is also important to recognize that different families will have different convictions about what clothing is modest. As you make decisions about what clothing is and is not appropriate for your child in their adolescent and teenage years, I recommend beginning with prayer, asking God to reveal any blind spots you may have in this area. It is easy to become so adjusted to the standards of the world that we become blinded to what truly honors God. So beginning with prayer is important. I also recommend that you discuss with your child that different people have different convictions about what is modest and what is immodest. Their friends' families may have different convictions about what is and is not appropriate to wear and, at least in most situations, it's not your child's job to tell other people if their clothing isn't modest. If how their friends or others dress is something they are concerned about, encourage them to talk with you about it. It is also wise to explain that when your child grows, he or she may have different convictions and choose to dress differently than the standards you set in your house, and that is okay. However, it is important to make clear that while they are living in your home, it is your job to set the standards for what they can and cannot wear.

As you wrap up the conversations about modesty, it is also important to remind our children of the goodness of the gospel. We should remind them that, on our own, we cannot perfectly reflect God by obeying his commands. But the amazing news is that Jesus took our sin upon himself and bore the full weight of God's wrath. Once we have turned from that sin and trusted in Jesus, we are clothed in his righteousness, and his Holy Spirit empowers us to obey him. Yes, we should strive to obey him in all areas, including modesty. But such striving should be done out of love for God and gratitude for what he accomplished for us through Jesus, not out of an effort to earn God's favor. This is understanding modesty within the context of the gospel.

• • •

Modesty can be a thorny topic to cover, especially after the confusing messages many of us grew up with in purity culture. However, as with all areas of sexuality, it need not be. If we ground these conversations in Scripture, we can help our children think and live biblically as they approach modesty in speech, conduct, and dress.

38

WHAT SHOULD I DO WHEN MY CHILD DEVELOPS A CRUSH?

Depending on your child's personality and makeup, they may begin to develop crushes as early as preschool or as late as middle school (or anywhere in between). Whenever this happens, it can be confusing to know what to do. In one sense, you may feel happy that your child gets to experience a sweet and innocent crush. But, on the other hand, you know it is unwise for them to begin focusing on romantic relationships this early in life. So what should you do? How can you help your child think biblically through innocent childhood crushes? I think the answer to this question involves intentionally avoiding two extremes: denial and encouragement.

DENIAL

As a third-grade teacher, I used to make a mistake that I see some parents make, which is to shut down any talk of crushes among children by saying, "Nope, you're way too young to date, so we're not going to talk about this right now." The intentions behind this sentiment are good. It's true that we don't want to encourage children to fixate on dating or marriage when that's something they're still too young to pursue. However, this isn't the wisest response. Rather than modeling how to recognize that some of our feelings point us to God's good design, this response encourages children to ignore and suppress their feelings.

Being drawn to a member of the opposite sex is part of God's good design. These feelings of attraction are part of what draws us to marriage and eventually lead husbands and wives to start families. So we don't want to dismiss these feelings or unintentionally teach our children that crushes and romantic interests are shameful or embarrassing.

ENCOURAGEMENT

On the opposite end of the spectrum, I've also seen parents make the mistake of encouraging their young children to pursue a crush by frequently talking about this person or planning opportunities for their child to interact with them. This approach is also harmful. Romance can certainly be a good gift from God, but we don't want to encourage our children to falsely believe that romantic feelings are the most important and exciting thing we can pursue. This isn't true or biblical. Romantic feelings ebb and flow, and putting too much stock in them is unwise.

I have also seen some well-meaning parents view talking about crushes as a way to build a closer relationship with their child. However, not only does doing this encourage an unhealthy view of romance in our children, but it can also ultimately hinder our relationship with them. Being too inquisitive about something your child might feel shy about discussing can build up a wall that makes your child want to share less. If your child shares with you that they have a crush, or if you figure it out on your own, you'll want to handle this conversation in a way that makes them feel safe sharing their feelings with you but will also point them in a healthy and biblical direction.

ADDRESSING CRUSHES WITH WISDOM

So how should you help your child navigate having romantic feelings when he or she is still too young to seriously think about a romantic relationship? I recommend that you start the conversation by explaining that these feelings are something to be grateful for. You can say, "These feelings you have are a gift from God. When you're old enough, these feelings will hopefully one day lead you to get married and start a family with someone who loves you and loves God. Because of that we can thank God for these feelings."

After this, you can gently remind your child that their focus should not be on romance. They are still too young to date and pursue marriage. Instead, you can talk about how their focus should be on caring for that person as a friend and a fellow image-bearer. Even as they grow into teenagers and young adults who are beginning to date and develop romantic relationships, it's still wise to teach them that their top priority should be loving and caring for the other person as a fellow image-bearer.

I would also encourage you to talk with your child about what qualities make a good spouse. Traits like patience, kindness, faithfulness, and selflessness are praiseworthy qualities your child should one day look for in a husband or wife. Such conversations can happen outside of the context of talking about crushes. However, when the topic of having a crush comes up, you can connect these two things and talk about how romantic feelings should draw your child toward someone who has qualities that would make them a good spouse. If you're married, praise the good qualities that you see in your spouse, and help your child see how these qualities are part of what makes your spouse such a good husband or wife. For example, if you see your husband taking out the trash, you can praise this act of service and point out to your child how having a servant's heart is one quality that makes a good spouse. If you see your wife being extra patient with a younger child, you can praise this patience and point out to your child that patience is a good thing to look for in a spouse. This will help your child understand that looking for a spouse should be about more than just looking for someone who gives them butterflies. It should also be about looking for someone who demonstrates God-honoring character.

One last thing to think about: in today's culture, so many things are overly sexualized, including friendship. Friendship is a beautiful gift from God, but it is a concept that's getting lost in this day and age. Many verses in Proverbs discuss the goodness of friendship and how to choose friends wisely (Proverbs 17:17; 27:6; 27:9; 27:17), and as parents, we want to encourage our children to develop strong, God-honoring friendships. So when our children become friends with someone of the opposite sex, it is important not to tease them about having a crush on that person or someday marrying them. At this stage, we want to encourage our children to focus on the goodness of God's gift of friendship and not feed into the world's view of sexualizing every relationship.

• • •

Our children will begin to develop romantic interests in others at some point in their development. When we avoid the extremes of denying these feelings and unwisely encouraging them, we can help our children view such feelings biblically and focus their attention on developing strong, healthy friendships.

39

WHAT DO I DO ABOUT THE LIBRARY HAVING SO MANY BOOKS PROMOTING LGBTQ+ IDEOLOGY?

When I was growing up, going to the library was one of my favorite activities. I loved wandering through the aisles, browsing the shelves, and picking out a stack of books to bring home. As an aunt, I now enjoy trips to the library with my nieces and nephews. However, such trips have changed a bit since my childhood. No longer is it safe to assume that any book a child picks up off the shelf is appropriate to bring home and read. Libraries across the country are filled with books overtly pushing the LGBTQ+ agenda, as well as books that subtly slip in characters and storylines promoting those same themes. This can make library trips stressful and confusing. What should we do when we are at the library and our children pick up books promoting LGBTQ+ ideology?

As I have mentioned in previous chapters, we always want to begin by focusing on what is good, true, and beautiful. In this case, I recommend first finding several authors and book series that do not push unbiblical ideas about sex and gender. Then, when you go to the library, you and your child can head to these books first and choose a few to check out. If you need recommendations for books like this, I highly recommend that you check out our book club at Foundation Worldview. We send out a monthly book club email with suggested books for children ages four through twelve. We also include corresponding worldview questions to discuss with your child. Another helpful resource is the *Read Aloud Revival* podcast and website, which recommends quality books for you and your child to read together.

As you seek to train your child to focus on what is good and true and beautiful, I would encourage you to read through (and potentially memorize) Philippians 4:8:

> Finally, brothers, whatever is true, whatever is honorable, whatever is
> just, whatever is pure, whatever is lovely, whatever is commendable,
> if there is any excellence, if there is anything worthy of praise, think
> about these things.

As you read this verse together, you can discuss what books you have read that fit this description. You can also discuss any books you have read—or chosen not to read—that don't fall into this category. This is where you can introduce the topic of books that do not align with God's good design for sexuality. You can explain that because of sin, there will be many times when we find books that do not follow God's good design. Then you can explain that whenever your child finds such books, they should remind themselves of the truth and then tell you about what they encountered in the book. Proactively training your child in this way will prepare them with a game plan for what to do anytime they encounter content that deviates from God's good design, whether you are there with them or not.

Still, the question remains: what should we do when our children encounter library books pushing LGBTQ+ ideology? Obviously, we should not encourage our children to read these books. However, it is also important that we don't freak out if our children pick up such books or ask to check them out. If we react strongly out of fear or anger and snatch the book away from our child, this reaction will cause panic in some children and unhealthy curiosity in others. So rather than panicking, we have two wise options to choose from: the first is to discuss why we are not going to read this book, and the second is to read the book together. Let's walk through both options.

Option number one is to discuss why you will not be reading the book. Here's a model conversation you could have: "Thank you so much for bringing this book to me. Let's look at this cover together. What do you see? Do you see how there's a family in this book? Who is part of this family?" Give your child time to evaluate the cover and point out why this book is different from the ones you would normally read. This gives them the opportunity to develop discernment. Then you can say, "That's right, instead of showing a family with a mommy and a daddy, this book shows a family with two daddies. Hmm. So is this book focusing on God's good design? Or is it focusing on something that doesn't match that design?" Give your child an opportunity to respond and then ask, "Can you remember what truth we should remind ourselves of if we see a book like this with two daddies?" And then together, you can quietly say, "God designed marriage to be one man and one woman becoming one flesh for life. God's design is so good." Wrap up the conversation by saying, "Since this book is not focusing on God's good design, we're not going to read it today. Please put it back on the shelf and pick out a different book instead."

Option number two is to read the book with your child and help them evaluate it. First, I recommend that you take the book home and read through it on your own before reading it with your child. If you determine that it is a good book to help your child develop discernment, set aside time to read through the book and discuss it. Here is a model of a conversation you could have about this book: "Before we turn the page, let's think about what we just read. This book says that the little boy's mommy and daddy don't know whether he's a boy or a girl. This book says that only the boy can tell them if he is a boy or a girl. Is that true?" Give your child an opportunity to think through the question, and then say, "No, this idea is not true. Can you remember what the truth is about whether we are a boy or a girl?" And together, you can say, "God designed us as male or female. God's design for us is so good." Then you can explain, "What this book is teaching is not right. It says that only this little boy knows if he's a boy or a girl. But the truth is, that little boy doesn't get to choose. God designed him as a little boy."

Whether you choose option one or option two depends on several factors: your child, their developmental stage, and what book they've picked up. I would encourage you not to always default to one option over the other. If we always say no to books with unbiblical agendas, we miss out on powerful opportunities to teach our children discernment. Yet, conversely, if we always engage with books that contain unbiblical agendas, we risk overexposing our children to ideas that do not align with God's good design for sex, gender, marriage, and family. The vast majority of content our children engage with should align with Philippians 4:8. So I highly encourage you to be discerning and prayerful about the books you engage with and the books you put down.

Most of what we have discussed in this chapter pertains to children under the age of ten. However, as your child grows, you can continue these patterns with the chapter books, comics, and novels they want to read. I suggest that you research the books your child brings home from the library. Focus on the Family's Plugged-In website reviews books from a Christian perspective, and a book's Amazon and Goodreads reviews can help give you an idea of what ideologies your child will encounter in these books.[1] Especially when your child hits middle school, they will likely encounter many books written for children their age that promote unbiblical ideas about sexuality and gender. You will want to continue training them to carefully evaluate the ideas presented in each book. Additionally, some books marketed to younger teens contain explicit content. In these cases, our children should *never* engage with this content, and we would be wise to work to have such content removed from the library. However, if the content is not explicit, reading and discussing a book with your child can be both instructive and relationship-building. You may want to consider having a book club–style conversation with your child that allows them to share their thoughts on the book and also gives you insight into how they are understanding and applying God's good design in their own life.

· · ·

Having to approach library trips with such intentionality and caution can feel overwhelming. However, as we ground our children in the goodness of God's design, we are preparing them to critically and biblically evaluate the content they will encounter on the library shelves and the pages of each book.

40

WHAT GUARDRAILS SHOULD I PUT IN PLACE WHEN IT COMES TO BOOKS, TV, INTERNET, AND OTHER MEDIA?

Media is one of the main ways our children are exposed to deviations from God's good design for sexuality. Even many seemingly innocent children's shows have begun depicting same-sex relationships and transgender or nonbinary characters. As parents, it may be tempting to prohibit all forms of media in our homes, but doing so will make it so we do not have opportunities to train our children to critically evaluate media messages. Instead, we should put up guardrails that train our children to make wise decisions when it comes to the media they consume. I think that three general principles should guide the guardrails we put in place.

PRINCIPLE 1: FORBID WHAT IS VILE

The first principle we should have in place is to forbid anything vile from entering our homes. Ephesians 5:1-5 and 11-12 says,

> Be imitators of God, as beloved children. And walk in love, as Christ loved us and gave himself up for us, a fragrant offering and sacrifice

to God. But sexual immorality and all impurity or covetousness must not even be named among you, as is proper among saints. Let there be no filthiness nor foolish talk nor crude joking, which are out of place, but instead let there be thanksgiving. For you may be sure of this, that everyone who is sexually immoral or impure, or who is covetous (that is, an idolater), has no inheritance in the kingdom of Christ and God... Take no part in the unfruitful works of darkness, but instead expose them. For it is shameful even to speak of the things that they do in secret.

We see from this passage that whatever is vile—whatever is upholding sexual immorality, impurity, covetousness, crude joking, foolish talk, or idolatry—has no place among Christians. These things should not be welcomed into our homes. Obviously, pornography and erotica (literature written for the purpose of arousal) fall into this category. Yet, other media that is not sexually explicit can also fall into this category if it boldly promotes ideas that God calls sin.

PRINCIPLE 2: EQUIP OUR CHILDREN TO THINK CRITICALLY

The second principle is to equip our children to think critically through the media they consume. After we've eliminated everything vile, what remains will be a mixed bag of books, shows, and movies that include both biblical and unbiblical ideas, and we need to equip our children to discern between the two. One passage of Scripture that speaks to this is Colossians 2:6-10, which says,

Therefore, as you received Christ Jesus the Lord, so walk in him, rooted and built up in him and established in the faith, just as you were taught, abounding in thanksgiving. See to it that no one takes you captive by philosophy and empty deceit, according to human tradition, according to the elemental spirits of the world, and not according to Christ. For in him the whole fullness of deity dwells bodily, and you have been filled in him, who is the head of all rule and authority.

We should seek to equip our children to stand firm in the Christian world-view by training them to carefully evaluate every idea that comes their way.

To do this, there are several key questions we can teach our children to ask as they engage in different forms of media:

1. **What is this author, producer, or artist's view of humans?** We should train our children to discern whether the content creator views humans as purposeful creations of God or the accidental result of blind, unguided evolution. Our children should also be able to discern whether the content creator presents humans as having inherent value and purpose given to them by God or as the creators of their own subjective value and purpose.

2. **What is this author, producer, or artist upholding as good?** Our children should also be equipped to recognize the ideas the content creator promotes as good. Our children should then be able to discern whether these ideas line up with what God has called good or whether they contradict it.

3. **What does this author, producer, or artist depict as evil?** Conversely, our children should be equipped to recognize the ideas the creator promotes as evil. This can be a particularly difficult skill to learn. So many modern forms of media now promote the idea that anyone or anything that stops someone from pursuing their desires is evil. But this contradicts what God has revealed in Scripture—that our desires often stem from our fallen nature (Jeremiah 17:9).

4. **Where does this author, producer, or artist express views or ideas that align with Scripture or those that contradict it?** This is where our children need to know Scripture, and not just isolated verses or stories. They need to know the entirety of God's Word to hold up every idea against it and evaluate whether that idea aligns with Scripture or contradicts it. (If your child is eight or older, I highly recommend you check out our Comparative Worldview

and Studying the Bible curricula at Foundation Worldview. These resources will train your children in both biblical literacy and biblical discernment.)

PRINCIPLE 3: FOCUS ON CONTENT THAT ALIGNS WITH PHILIPPIANS 4:8

The third principle is to spend most of our time focusing on what aligns with Philippians 4:8: "Whatever is true, whatever is honorable, whatever is just, whatever is pure, whatever is lovely, whatever is commendable, if there is any excellence, if there is anything worthy of praise, think about these things." I recommend memorizing this verse with your child and having regular conversations discussing what it means for something to fall within this category.

I would also encourage you to evaluate, as a family, what amount of your media consumption is spent on Philippians 4:8 material and what percentage is not. You can sit down and make a list of what shows, movies, music, books, and other types of content, that you're consuming as a family, and then ask of each item, "Does this ultimately align with Philippians 4:8? Or are there too many pieces that do not?" If you determine that less than 50 percent of your family media time is spent engaging with content that aligns with Philippians 4:8, I highly encourage making a plan to change that. The media we consume is a lot like our physical diet; there can be room for some junk food here and there, but we need to make it our goal to dedicate most of our diet to what will truly nourish. If most of the media we consume does not align with Philippians 4:8, we and our children will begin to be rooted in a worldview that contradicts Scripture. Our families' spiritual health will suffer because we're spending too much time on junk food media.

• • •

It is easy to begin mindlessly consuming media in a world where it is present everywhere. However, putting wise media guardrails in place will help protect our children from what is vile, train them to carefully evaluate ideas, and cultivate an appetite for what is good.

CONCLUSION

Well, friend, we've made it! Can you believe it? Throughout the pages of this book, we have explored 40 foundational conversations to have with our children about God's good design for sexuality and gender. I know that some of the topics we covered were challenging, but I hope that as you've read these chapters, your eyes have been opened to how important it is to have these discussions before our children receive faulty messages from the world. Thank you for investing time to explore, consider, and implement these vital conversations.

As you move forward in parenting, please remember that none of these discussions are a one-and-done deal. Most are talks you'll end up repeating and revisiting with your child many times over the years to come. With each conversation, your goal isn't to get everything perfect once and for all but to develop a foundation of truth that grows sturdier as you continue to disciple your child. As you seek ways to reinforce these concepts, encourage your child to bring their questions to you. As they encounter everyday situations in the world around them, and even within their own heart and mind, you'll have many more opportunities to continue guiding their understanding of God's good design for sex. And remember, even if you don't word things correctly or you have a reaction that isn't the wisest, this too provides an opportunity for discipleship. Mistakes give you a chance to come to your child again and say, "Actually, I made a mistake the last time we talked about this. Can we talk about it more?"

At times, you may feel confused or even frustrated by the need to repeat the same information in these discussions with your child. However, remember that this is what's to be expected. Children learn through repetition, so it may take several similar conversations for them to remember the basics of sex and anatomy, and many more to truly understand God's good design for this part of our lives. The need for such repetition need not be frustrating. Instead, it can encourage us to reflect God's kindness toward us, his children. During Jesus's earthly ministry, he spent three short years teaching, training, and modeling for his disciples how they were to live. Throughout the gospels, we see these men repeatedly struggle to grasp Jesus's teachings, needing continual reminders and further explanations. Yet Jesus patiently and persistently guided, encouraged, and corrected his disciples. Similarly, God has given you eighteen short years with your child. And just as the disciples needed to hear the same concepts over and over and over before such teachings finally took root in their hearts and minds, so will your child. So let's seek to follow Jesus's example of patiently guiding, encouraging, and correcting our children as they seek to understand and follow God's good design.

As your child grows into their teen years, these conversations will also need to grow to cover more information. Talking with teens is beyond the scope of my expertise, but the following resources can help guide you through some of these conversations:

- *Facing the Facts: The Truth About God, Sex, and You* by Stan and Brenna Jones

- *Relationships: 11 Lessons to Give Kids a Greater Understanding of Biblical Sexuality* by Luke and Trisha Gilkerson

- *Across the Kitchen Table: Talking About Trans with Your Teen* by Sam A. Andreades

- *Why Does God Care Who I Sleep With* by Sam Allberry

Even though you won't want to use the 40 questions discussed here as an exact template for how to talk about sexuality and gender with your teen, remember that the principles we've covered in this book still apply to such conversations. Start with the positive biblically sound theology. Then move on to how sin has corrupted God's design. Ask your older child questions. Seek to genuinely listen. Don't freak out over their questions, but respond patiently, knowing it is okay to say, "That is a great question. I don't know the answer right now, but I promise to do some research and get back to you soon." If something they share leaves you shocked or upset, do everything you can to respond with grace and tenderness. And, finally, remember to pray!

Speaking of prayer, as we close our time together, I would like to spend a moment praying over you and your child as you leave the pages of this book and continue on the journey of parenting. If it's helpful for you, please feel free to personalize this prayer and pray it over yourself and your family as you're preparing to have these conversations.

Father, I come before you with a heart full of gratitude for who you are and all that you have done to reconcile us to yourself. I lift before you, this dear reader. Please guide them as they seek to faithfully represent you and your good design to their child. Please give them the words and wisdom they need for these conversations, and provide them with insight into the heart and mind of their child. Please strengthen them to trust you and continue seeking you when they find that parenting through these conversations becomes challenging. Above all, please give them an ever-increasing hunger for you, ground them deeply in your Word, and strengthen them to trust that you will use every situation they face in parenting for your glory and their good.

I also ask that you would have your hand on their child. If that child does not yet know you, please work in their heart, convicting them of their sin and their need for you. Please give them a hunger for your Word and your ways. As this child engages with their parent in these conversations about sexuality and gender, please open their eyes to the goodness of your design. Please protect them from the evils of pornography, abuse, and every other vile sexual corruption. As they grow and begin to experience sexual desires and longings, please help them discern between longings that stem from your good design and those that stem from their fallen flesh. Above all, please let them desire the consummation of the grand story to which all sexuality was designed to point, the Marriage Supper of the Lamb. We love you, Father, and pray all of these things in the mighty name of your Son, Jesus. Amen.

Well, my friend, this is the end of our journey together. Thank you so much for sticking through it with me. Though I dare not pretend to have the answers to all questions about raising children with a biblical understanding of sexuality, if my team and I can be of help as you encounter different situations with your child, please do not hesitate to reach out to us at FoundationWorldview.com. I am praying for you and grateful for you.

With joy and gratitude,
Elizabeth

NOTES

7. HOW DO I HELP MY CHILD UNDERSTAND WHY SEX IS ONLY FOR MARRIAGE?

1. Medical Institute for Sexual Health, "The Brain and Sex," accessed March 28, 2025, https://www.med institute.org/the-brain-and-sex/.

2. Jane Anderson, "The Impact of Family Structure on the Health of Children: Effects of Divorce," *The Linacre Quarterly*, vol. 81, no. 4 (2014): 378-387, doi: 10.1179/0024363914Z.00000000087. Melissa S. Kearney, "The U.S. Economy Needs More Two Parent Families," *Time*, September 28, 2023, https://time.com/6317692/u-s-economy-two-parent-families/.

8. HOW CAN I HELP MY CHILD THINK BIBLICALLY ABOUT THEIR BODY?

1. James Krzymowski, "The Link Between Social Media and Body Image Issues Among Youth in the United States, Ballard Brief, Winter 2024, https://ballardbrief.byu.edu/issue-briefs/the-link-between-social-media-and-body-image-issues-among-youth-in-the-united-states. Gary Goldfield, "Reducing Social Media Use Significantly Improves Body Image in Teens, Young Adults," American Psychological Association, February 23, 2023, https://www.apa.org/news/press/releases/2023/02/social-media-body-image. Harvard T. H. Chan School of Public Health, "Exploring the Effect of Social Media on Teen Girls' Mental Health," September 14, 2023, https://www.hsph.harvard.edu/news/hsph-in-the-news/exploring-the-effect-of-social-media-on-teen-girls-mental-health/.

2. For more information on Screenstrong, visit https://screenstrong.org/.

3. Jonathan Morrow, "Refresh Roadmap: A Practical Guide for Parents to Navigate Screen Time and Social Media with Confidence," https://resources.jonathanmorrow.org/offers/7S4XLVJk/checkout.

9. HOW DO I TALK TO MY CHILD ABOUT THE NEGATIVE CONSEQUENCES OF SEX OUTSIDE OF MARRIAGE?

1. Cleveland Clinic, "Sexually Transmitted Infections," https://my.clevelandclinic.org/health/diseases/9138-sexually-transmitted-diseases--infections-stds--stis. Mayo Clinic, "Sexually Transmitted Diseases (STDs)," https://www.mayoclinic.org/diseases-conditions/sexually-transmitted-diseases-stds/symptoms-causes/syc-20351240.

11. HOW DO I TALK WITH MY CHILD ABOUT MASTURBATION FROM A BIBLICAL PERSPECTIVE?

1. Future of Sex Education, "National Sex Education Standards: Core Content and Skills," K-12, 2nd ed., https://advocatesforyouth.org/wp-content/uploads/2020/03/NSES-2020-web.pdf. See these standards on pages 20 and 43.

2. *Merriam-Webster Dictionary*, "masturbation," https://www.merriam-webster.com/dictionary/masturbation.

3. Dr. Freda Bush and Dr. Joe McIlhaney, "Hooked: The Bonding Power of Sex," Family Life, https://www.family life.com/articles/topics/parenting/parenting-challenges/sexual-wholeness/hooked-the-bonding-power-of-sex/.

12. HOW DO I TALK TO MY CHILD ABOUT PORNOGRAPHY?

1. For more on the pervasiveness of pornography, see Novus Project, http://thenovusproject.org/resource-hub/parents.

2. Lyndon Azcuna, "The Porn Pandemic," LifePlan, October 28, 2021, https://www.lifeplan.org/the-porn-pandemic/.

3. American College of Pediatricians, "The Impact of Pornography on Children," https://acpeds.org/position-statements/the-impact-of-pornography-on-children.

4. Fight the New Drug, "What's the Average Age of a Child's First Exposure to Porn?," https://fightthenew drug.org/real-average-age-of-first-exposure/.

14. HOW DO I TALK TO MY CHILD ABOUT WHAT THE BIBLE TEACHES ABOUT GENDER IDENTITY AND TRANSGENDERISM?

1. *Merriam-Webster Dictionary*, "gender identity," https://www.merriam-webster.com/dictionary/gender%20 identity.

2. American Psychological Association, "Understanding Transgender People, Gender Identity and Gender Expression," updated July 8, 2024, https://www.apa.org/topics/lgbtq/transgender-people-gender-identity-gender-expression.

16. WILL TALKING WITH MY CHILD ABOUT SEX AT A YOUNG AGE STEAL THEIR INNOCENCE?

1. *Merriam-Webster Dictionary*, "innocence," https://www.merriam-webster.com/dictionary/innocence.

2. I would also recommend this biblical counseling center that offers virtual appointments: https://biblical counselingcenter.org/.

20. AM I HYPOCRITICAL IF I TEACH MY CHILD THE BIBLICAL DESIGN FOR SEX, EVEN THOUGH I DID NOT FOLLOW IT?

1. *Merriam-Webster Dictionary*, "hypocrisy," https://www.merriam-webster.com/dictionary/hypocrisy.

22. WHAT CAN I DO TO HELP PROTECT MY CHILD FROM SEXUAL ABUSE?

1. Darkness to Light, "The Issue of Child Sexual Abuse," https://www.d2l.org/wp-content/uploads/2023/03/Child-Sexual-Abuse-Statistics_The-Issue.pdf.

2. For more information on spotting signs of sexual abuse, I recommend that you check out Focus on the Family's resources. They have a host of articles and other resources on sexual abuse and what signs to look for in our children.

23. WHAT DO I NEED TO TEACH MY CHILD ABOUT CONSENT?

1. *Merriam-Webster Dictionary*, "consent," https://www.merriam-webster.com/dictionary/consent.

2. Debby Herbenick, et al., "Diverse Sexual Behaviors and Pornography Use: Findings From a Nationally Representative Probability Survey of Americans Aged 18 to 60 Years," *The Journal of Sexual Medicine* vol. 17, no. 4 (2020): 623-633, doi: 10.1016/j.jsxm.2020.01.013.

3. Debby Herbenick, et al., "'It Was Scary, But Then it Was Kind of Exciting': Young Women's Experiences with Choking During Sex," *Archives of Sexual Behavior* vol. 51, no. 2 (2021): 1103-1123, doi: 10.1007/s10508-021-02049-x.

4. For more on this topic, see Joe Carter, "Violent Pornography's Assault on the Marriage Bed," The Gospel Coalition, May 20, 2024, https://www.thegospelcoalition.org/article/violent-pornographys-marriage/.

24. HOW DO I TEACH MY CHILD TO LOVE OTHERS WITHOUT AFFIRMING ANOTHER PERSON'S SIN?

1. *Sense and Sensibility*, produced by the BBC, March 30, 2008.

25. HOW SHOULD I GUIDE MY CHILD IF THEIR FRIEND COMES OUT AS GAY, LESBIAN, OR TRANSGENDER?

1. Jeffrey M. Jones, "LGBTQ+ Identification in U.S. Now at 7.6%," Gallup, March 13, 2024, https://news.gallup.com/poll/611864/lgbtq-identification.aspx. Justin McCarthy and Rachael Yi, "LGBTQ+ Adults are Coming Out at Younger Ages Than in the Past," Gallup, July 26, 2024, https://news.gallup.com/poll/647636/lgbtq-adults-coming-younger-ages-past.aspx.

28. HOW DO I PREPARE MY CHILD TO INTERACT WITH A FAMILY MEMBER OR FRIEND WHO IS TRANSITIONING?

1. Jody L. Herman, Andrew R. Flores, and Kathryn K. O'Neill, "How Many Adults and Youth Identify as Transgender in the United States?" UCLA School of Law Williams Institute, June 2022, https://williamsinstitute.law.ucla.edu/publications/trans-adults-united-states/

32. HOW SHOULD I EXPLAIN SEXUALLY CHARGED TERMS LIKE *HOT* AND *SEXY*?

1. *Merriam-Webster Dictionary*, "hot," 2.b, https://www.merriam-webster.com/dictionary/hot, and "sexy," https://www.merriam-webster.com/dictionary/sexy.

2. Douglas Kaine McKelvey, *Every Moment Holy: Volume 1* (Rabbit Room Press, 2017), 248.

36. HOW CAN I ENCOURAGE MY CHILD WHO DOESN'T FIT IN WITH TRADITIONAL GENDER NORMS?

1. The passage in Timothy addresses women through verse 15. However, verses 11 through 15 can be confusing. For a thorough treatment of them, I recommend seeing Mike Winger's *Women in Ministry* series on YouTube.

37. HOW DO I ENCOURAGE SEXUAL MODESTY IN MY CHILD WITHOUT INTRODUCING SHAME?

1. *Merriam-Webster Dictionary*, "modesty," https://www.merriam-webster.com/dictionary/modesty.

39. WHAT DO I DO ABOUT THE LIBRARY HAVING SO MANY BOOKS PROMOTING LGBTQ+ IDEOLOGY?

1. For more information on Pluggedin's reviews of books, visit their site at https://www.pluggedin.com/books/.

ACKNOWLEDGMENTS

Writing a book was something I said I would never do. "I'm not a writer," I'd told myself hundreds of times. However, I've learned over the years that I end up doing most of the things I say I'll never do. (So let me now officially announce I will never meet and marry the man of my dreams, earn enough money to give more than 50 percent of my income to missions, or spend a few weeks vacationing in Hawaii.) In all seriousness, though, this book exists thanks to the persistence and patience of the Harvest House team, specifically Sherrie Slopianka and Don Sage, who continued to encourage me to write, even after I said, "No, thanks. I'm not a writer," time after time. Thank you, Sherrie and Don, for seeing the potential in this project and in me even before I could.

This book also would not exist without my wonderful editors, Emma Saisslin and Audrey Greeson. Emma, thank you for the hundreds of hours you invested pouring over Foundation Worldview podcast transcripts to help me identify the key ideas pertaining to each chapter. Thank you for your honest critiques and encouragement and for providing the perspective of those one generation below me. Your insights have been of immense value. Audrey, thank you for hanging in there with me for multiple years as we narrowed down the focus of this book. Thank you for lending your perspective both as a mom of young children and a theologian. Having your expertise in theology has put my mind at ease many times as I've wrestled with how to phrase things in simple yet theologically accurate terms.

I am also grateful to my teammates at Foundation Worldview—Danielle King, Jenny Stillman, Jonathan Matlock, Pam Porter, Renee Reithel, and Taliah Kendrick. Your insight into everything from the topics covered to the design of the cover has made this book a project that will both equip parents and faithfully represent our mission and vision at Foundation Worldview.

I am also grateful for the host of family and friends who let me bounce ideas off them as I tweaked the content in this book—Rebecca and Terry Morrow, Rachel and Tom Schmidt, Danielle and Seth King, Jenny and Christian Stillman, and Steph and Dan Tsouloufis. Thank you for being faithful friends who love me with the love of Christ, encourage me, and are bold enough to tell me when I am wrong.

Though my parents, Joe and Karen Urbanowicz, were not involved in the writing process, this book would not exist without their faithful discipleship during my formative years. Thank you, Mom and Dad, for teaching me to love God, love his Word, and understand the beauty of his good design. I love you, and I am so thankful God blessed me with you as parents!

Ultimately, this book exists because of God's faithfulness. As Colossians 1:15-18 makes clear, all things exist and are sustained because of his kindness. And, without his unmerited favor, Harvest House never would have pursued me to write this book. (As I mentioned before, I'm not a writer.) It is my prayer that this book would not only be used to guide parents through foundational conversations but that each page would leave the reader in greater awe of the goodness of God and his design, longing for the day when the grand story to which sexuality was designed to point comes to fruition (Revelation 19:6-9). Come, Lord Jesus!

ABOUT THE AUTHOR

Elizabeth Urbanowicz holds an MSEd from Northern Illinois University in Literacy Education and an MA in Christian Apologetics from Biola University. She began her career as an elementary teacher in a Christian school before she founded Foundation Worldview, where she now works full-time on developing comparative worldview and apologetics resources for children. Her goal is to prepare the next generation to be lifelong critical thinkers and lifelong disciples of Jesus Christ. Connect with Elizabeth at FoundationWorldview.com.

To learn more about our Harvest Apologetics resources, please visit:

www.HarvestApologetics.com

HARVEST APOLOGETICS
An Imprint of Harvest House Publishers